BOB P

FIND IT
in the
BIBLE
FOR WOMEN

Lists, Lists, and more Lists

HOWARD BOOKS
A DIVISION OF SIMON & SCHUSTER
New York London Toronto Sydney

Our purpose at Howard Books is to:

- *Increase faith* in the hearts of growing Christians
- *Inspire holiness* in the lives of believers
- *Instill hope* in the hearts of struggling people everywhere

Because He's coming again!

HOWARD BOOKS

Published by Howard Books, a division of Simon & Schuster, Inc.
1230 Avenue of the Americas, New York, NY 10020
www.howardpublishing.com

Find It in the Bible for Women © 2007 by Bob Phillips

10 Digit ISBN: 1-58229-640-5; 13 Digit ISBN: 978-1-58229-640-1

10 9 8 7 6 5 4 3 2

HOWARD colophon is a registered trademark of Simon & Schuster, Inc.

Manufactured in the United States of America

For information regarding special discounts for bulk purchases, please contact: Simon & Schuster Special Sales at 1-800-456-6798 or business@simonandschuster.com.

Edited by Between the Lines
Cover design by UDG Design Works
Interior design by Stephanie D. Walker

■ CONTENTS

CONTENTS

THE BIBLE

What book is that whose page divine
Bears God's impress on every line,
And in man's soul makes light to shine?
The Bible

When sin and sorrow, want and woe,
Assail poor mortals here below,
What book can then true comfort show?
The Bible

What paints the beautiful and true,
And mirrors at a single view
The paths which here we should pursue?
The Bible

What is the brightest gift the Lord
In his great mercy did award
To man, to be his shield and guard?
The Bible

What teaches love and truth and peace,
And bids good will 'mong men increase?
And bids strife, war and murder cease?
The Bible

Oh! What can make this world of woe
With peace and truth and virtue glow,
Till men no sin nor sorrow know?
The Bible

When error fled before its foes,
And Luther, like the morning, rose,
With what did he Rome's crimes expose?
The Bible

What is it now that baffles Rome,
Where error long has found a home,
In many a pagan pile and dome?
The Bible

What gives to man the power and will,
God's high behest to do fulfill
And points the way to Zion's hill?
The Bible

When death comes knocking at the door,
And man's short life on earth is o'er,
What tells of bliss for ever more?
The Bible

—Author Unknown

LIST #1

34 Character Traits of a Woman of Great Influence

Proverbs 31 gives a description of 34 character traits of a truly amazing, godly woman.

1. She is highly esteemed (v. 10).

2. She is valuable (v. 10).

3. She is worthy of her family's trust (v. 11).

4. She provides for her husband's needs (v. 11).

5. She is a positive influence (v. 12).

6. She is not idle (v. 13).

7. She is a hard worker (v. 13).

8. She is a good provider (v. 14).

9. She is disciplined (v. 15).

10. She is a servant (v. 15).

11. She is compassionate (v. 15).

12. She is savvy in business (v. 16).

13. She is visionary and wise as an investor (v. 16).

14. She is diligent (v. 17).

15. She is determined and tenacious (v. 17).

16. She is full of wisdom (v. 18).

17. She is full of energy (v. 18).

18. She is a multitasker (v. 19).

19. She has a giving, compassionate, and concerned spirit (v. 20).

20. She plans ahead (v. 21).

21. She cares about her home (v. 22).

22. She cares about her looks (v. 22).

23. She is an asset to her husband and helps him become successful (v. 23).

24. She is creative (v. 24).

25. She is a woman of virtue (v. 25).

26. She is full of confidence (v. 26).

27. She controls her tongue (v. 26).

28. She protects her home (v. 27).

29. She doesn't waste time (v. 27).

30. She is appreciated by her children (v. 28).

31. She is adored by her husband (vv. 28–29).

32. She understands the importance of a relationship with God (v. 30).

33. She is worthy of reward (v. 31).

34. She is to be respected for her words and deeds (v. 31).

# LIST #2
8 Principles for Overcoming Loneliness

It is possible to be around people and still feel lonely. Loneliness is a desolate emotion often accompanied by emotional pain, but God can fill any void that is left from feeling deserted.

1. "Have I not commanded you? Be strong and courageous. Do not be terrified; do not be discouraged, for the LORD your God will be with you wherever you go" (Joshua 1:9).

2. "Even though I walk through the valley of the shadow of death, I will fear no evil, for you are with me; your rod and your staff, they comfort me" (Psalm 23:4).

3. "Though my father and mother forsake me, the LORD will receive me" (Psalm 27:10).

4. "He will command his angels concerning you to guard you in all your ways" (Psalm 91:11).

5. "Do not fear, for I am with you; do not be dismayed, for I am your God. I will strengthen you and help you; I will uphold you with my righteous right hand" (Isaiah 41:10).

6. "This is what the LORD says—he who created you, O Jacob, he who formed you, O Israel: 'Fear not, for I have redeemed you; I have summoned you by name; you are mine. When you pass through the waters, I will be with you; and when you pass through the rivers, they will not sweep over you'" (Isaiah 43:1–2).

7. "Surely I am with you always, to the very end of the age" (Matthew 28:20).

8. "God has said, 'Never will I leave you; never will I forsake you.' So we say with confidence, 'The Lord is my helper; I will not be afraid. What can man do to me?'" (Hebrews 13:5–6).

LIST #3
15 Men Who Married More Than One Wife

One of the curiosities of the Bible is the number of men who had more than one wife.

1. Lamech
   - "Lamech married two women, one named Adah and the other Zillah" (Genesis 4:19).

2. Abraham
   - "After Abram had been living in Canaan ten years, Sarai his wife took her Egyptian maidservant Hagar and gave her to her husband to be his wife" (Genesis 16:3).
   - "Abraham took another wife, whose name was Keturah" (Genesis 25:1).

3. Esau
   - "When Esau was forty years old, he married Judith daughter of Beeri the Hittite, and also Basemath daughter of Elon the Hittite" (Genesis 26:34).
   - "Esau then realized how displeasing the Canaanite women were to his father Isaac; so he went to Ishmael and married Mahalath, the sister of Nebaioth and daughter of Ishmael son of Abraham, in addition to the wives he already had" (Genesis 28:8–9).

4. Jacob
   - "He [Jacob] finished the week with Leah, and then Laban gave him his daughter Rachel to be his wife" (Genesis 29:28).

- "[Rachel] gave him her servant Bilhah as a wife. Jacob slept with her, and she became pregnant and bore him a son" (Genesis 30:4–5).

- "When Leah saw that she had stopped having children, she took her maidservant Zilpah and gave her to Jacob as a wife" (Genesis 30:9).

5. Moses

- "After Moses had sent away his wife Zipporah, his father-in-law Jethro received her and her two sons" (Exodus 18:2–3).

- "Miriam and Aaron began to talk against Moses because of his Cushite wife, for he had married a Cushite" (Numbers 12:1).

6. Gideon

- "He had seventy sons of his own, for he had many wives" (Judges 8:30).

7. Elkanah

- "He had two wives; one was called Hannah and the other Peninnah" (1 Samuel 1:2).

8. Saul

- "His wife's name was Ahinoam daughter of Ahimaaz" (1 Samuel 14:50).

- "Saul had had a concubine named Rizpah" (2 Samuel 3:7).

9. David

- "I [God] gave your master's house to you, and your master's wives into your [David's] arms" (2 Samuel 12:8).

- David's wives names were Michal, Abigail, Ahinoam, Bathsheba, Maacah, Haggith, Abital, and Eglah (1 Samuel 25:42–44; 2 Samuel 3:2–5; 1 Chronicles 3:1–9).

10. Solomon
    - "He had seven hundred wives of royal birth and three hundred concubines, and his wives led him astray" (1 Kings 11:3).

11. Ahab
    - "The king of Israel [Ahab] summoned all the elders of the land and said to them, 'See how this man is looking for trouble! When he sent for my wives and my children, my silver and my gold, I did not refuse him'" (1 Kings 20:7).

12. Rehoboam
    - "Rehoboam loved Maacah daughter of Absalom more than any of his other wives and concubines. In all, he had eighteen wives and sixty concubines" (2 Chronicles 11:21).

13. Abijah
    - "Abijah grew in strength. He married fourteen wives and had twenty-two sons and sixteen daughters" (2 Chronicles 13:21).

14. Joash
    - "Jehoiada chose two wives for him [Joash], and he had sons and daughters" (2 Chronicles 24:3).

15. Xerxes
    - "On the seventh day, when King Xerxes was in high spirits from wine, he commanded the seven

eunuchs who served him—Mehuman, Biztha, Harbona, Bigtha, Abagtha, Zethar and Carcas—to bring before him Queen Vashti, wearing her royal crown, in order to display her beauty to the people and nobles, for she was lovely to look at" (Esther 1:10–11).

- "The king was attracted to Esther more than to any of the other women, and she won his favor and approval more than any of the other virgins. So he set a royal crown on her head and made her queen instead of Vashti" (Esther 2:17).

LIST #4
5 Healthy Self-Image Passages

Many people struggle with their self-image. They haven't made peace with themselves and accepted who they are. But God wants us to trust him and become who he has made us to be. Here are some passages to consider:

1. "The LORD does not look at the things man looks at. Man looks at the outward appearance, but the LORD looks at the heart" (1 Samuel 16:7).

2. "You created my inmost being; you knit me together in my mother's womb. I praise you because I am fearfully and wonderfully made; your works are wonderful, I know that full well. My frame was not hidden from you when I was made in the secret place. When I was woven together in the depths of the earth, your eyes saw my unformed body. All the days ordained for me were written in your book before one of them came to be" (Psalm 139:13–16).

3. "Praise be to the God and Father of our Lord Jesus Christ, who has blessed us in the heavenly realms with every spiritual blessing in Christ. For he chose us in him before the creation of the world to be holy and blameless in his sight. In love he predestined us to be adopted as his sons through Jesus Christ, in accordance with his pleasure and will—to the praise of his glorious grace, which he has freely given us in the One he loves" (Ephesians 1:3–6).

4. "He who began a good work in you will carry it on to completion until the day of Christ Jesus" (Philippians 1:6).

5. "Do nothing out of selfish ambition or vain conceit, but in humility consider others better than yourselves. Each of you should look not only to your own interests, but also to the interests of others. Your attitude should be the same as that of Christ Jesus" (Philippians 2:3–5).

◼ LIST #5

61 Encouragements for When You Have a Problem

Problems and difficulties are common to all humanity. God is aware and concerned about the situations you face, and his Word has some encouragement and comfort for you.

1. "Blessed is the man whom God corrects; so do not despise the discipline of the Almighty. For he wounds, but he also binds up; he injures, but his hands also heal" (Job 5:17–18).

2. "He knows the way that I take: when he has tested me, I will come forth as gold" (Job 23:10).

3. "I will lie down and sleep in peace, for you alone, O LORD make me dwell in safety" (Psalm 4:8).

4. "Let all who take refuge in you be glad; let them ever sing for joy. Spread your protection over them, that those who love your name may rejoice in you" (Psalm 5:11).

5. "The LORD is a refuge for the oppressed, a stronghold in times of trouble. Those who know your name will trust in you, for you, LORD, have never forsaken those who seek you" (Psalm 9:9–10).

6. "I have set the LORD always before me. Because he is at my right hand, I will not be shaken. Therefore my heart is glad and my tongue rejoices; my body also will rest secure, because you will not abandon me to the grave, nor will you let your Holy One see decay" (Psalm 16:8–10).

7. "The cords of death entangled me; the torrents of destruction overwhelmed me. The cords of the grave coiled around me; the snares of death confronted me. In my distress I called to the LORD; I cried to my God for help. From his temple he heard my voice; my cry came before him into his ears" (Psalm 18:4–6).

8. "Even though I walk through the valley of the shadow of death, I will fear no evil, for you are with me; your rod and your staff, they comfort me" (Psalm 23:4).

9. "The LORD is my light and my salvation—whom shall I fear? The LORD is the stronghold of my life—of whom shall I be afraid?" (Psalm 27:1).

10. "Though an army besiege me, my heart will not fear; though war break out against me, even then will I be confident" (Psalm 27:3).

11. "In the day of trouble he will keep me safe in his dwelling; he will hide me in the shelter of his tabernacle and set me high upon a rock. Then my head will be exalted above the enemies who surround me; at his tabernacle will I sacrifice with shouts of joy; I will sing and make music to the LORD" (Psalm 27:5–6).

12. "I am still confident of this: I will see the goodness of the LORD in the land of the living. Wait for the LORD; be strong and take heart and wait for the LORD" (Psalm 27:13–14).

13. "Praise be to the LORD, for he has heard my cry for mercy. The LORD is my strength and my shield; my heart trusts in him, and I am helped. My heart leaps for joy and I will give thanks to him in song" (Psalm 28:6–7).

14. "Sing to the LORD, you saints of his; praise his holy name. For his anger lasts only a moment, but his favor lasts a lifetime; weeping may remain for a night, but rejoicing comes in the morning" (Psalm 30:4–5).

15. "In you, O LORD, I have taken refuge; let me never be put to shame; deliver me in your righteousness. Turn your ear to me, come quickly to my rescue; be my rock of refuge, a strong fortress to save me. Since you are my rock and my fortress, for the sake of your name lead and guide me" (Psalm 31:1–3).

16. "I sought the LORD, and he answered me; he delivered me from all my fears" (Psalm 34:4).

17. "A righteous man may have many troubles, but the LORD delivers him from them all; he protects all his bones, not one of them will be broken" (Psalm 34:19–20).

18. "If the LORD delights in a man's way, he makes his steps firm; though he stumble, he will not fall, for the LORD upholds him with his hand" (Psalm 37:23–24).

19. "Why are you downcast, O my soul? Why so disturbed within me? Put your hope in God, for I will yet praise him, my Savior and my God" (Psalm 42:5–6).

20. "God is our refuge and strength, an ever-present help in trouble. Therefore we will not fear, though the earth give way and the mountains fall into the heart of the sea, though its waters roar and foam and the mountains quake with their surging" (Psalm 46:1–3).

21. "Sacrifice thank offerings to God, fulfill your vows to the Most High, and call upon me in the day of trouble;

I will deliver you, and you will honor me" (Psalm 50:14–15).

22. "I call to God, and the LORD saves me. Evening, morning and noon I cry out in distress, and he hears my voice. He ransoms me unharmed from the battle waged against me, even though many oppose me" (Psalm 55:16–18).

23. "Cast your cares on the LORD and he will sustain you; he will never let the righteous fall" (Psalm 55:22).

24. "When I am afraid, I will trust in you. In God, whose word I praise, in God I trust; I will not be afraid. What can mortal man do to me?" (Psalm 56:3–4).

25. "Hear my cry, O God; listen to my prayer. From the ends of the earth I call to you, I call as my heart grows faint; lead me to the rock that is higher than I. For you have been my refuge, a strong tower against the foe. I long to dwell in your tent forever and take refuge in the shelter of your wings" (Psalm 61:1–4).

26. "My soul finds rest in God alone; my salvation comes from him. He alone is my rock and my salvation; he is my fortress, I will never be shaken" (Psalm 62:1–2).

27. "Find rest, O my soul, in God alone; my hope comes from him. He alone is my rock and my salvation; he is my fortress, I will not be shaken. My salvation and my honor depend on God; he is my mighty rock, my refuge. Trust in him at all times, O people; pour out your hearts to him, for God is our refuge" (Psalm 62:5–8).

28. "All mankind will fear; they will proclaim the works of God and ponder what he has done. Let the righteous

rejoice in the LORD and take refuge in him; let all the upright in heart praise him" (Psalm 64:9–10).

29. "In you, O LORD, I have taken refuge; let me never be put to shame. Rescue me and deliver me in your righteousness, turn your ear to me and save me. Be my rock of refuge, to which I can always go; give the command to save me, for you are my rock and my fortress" (Psalm 71:1–3).

30. "Whom have I in heaven but you? And earth has nothing I desire besides you. My flesh and my heart may fail, but God is the strength of my heart and my portion forever" (Psalm 73:25–26).

31. "The LORD God is a sun and shield; the LORD bestows favor and honor; no good thing does he withhold from those whose walk is blameless. O LORD Almighty, blessed is the man who trusts in you" (Psalm 84:11–12).

32. "Hear my prayer, O LORD; listen to my cry for mercy. In the day of my trouble I will call to you, for you will answer me" (Psalm 86:6–7).

33. "You, O Lord, are a compassionate and gracious God, slow to anger, abounding in love and faithfulness. Turn to me and have mercy on me; grant your strength to your servant and save the son of your maidservant. Give me a sign of your goodness, that my enemies may see it and be put to shame, for you, O LORD, have helped me and comforted me" (Psalm 86:15–17).

34. "Unless the LORD had given me help, I would soon have dwelt in the silence of death. When I said, 'My foot is slipping,' your love, O LORD, supported me.

When anxiety was great within me, your consolation brought joy to my soul" (Psalm 94:17–19).

35. "It was good for me to be afflicted so that I might learn your decrees. The law from your mouth is more precious to me than thousands of pieces of silver and gold" (Psalm 119:71–72).

36. "He heals the brokenhearted and binds up their wounds. He determines the number of the stars and calls them each by name. Great is our Lord and mighty in power; his understanding has no limit. The Lord sustains the humble but casts the wicked to the ground" (Psalm 147:3–6).

37. "My son, do not despise the Lord's discipline and do not resent his rebuke, because the Lord disciplines those he loves, as a father the son he delights in" (Proverbs 3:11–12).

38. "Do not fear, for I am with you; do not be dismayed, for I am your God. I will strengthen you and help you; I will uphold you with my righteous right hand" (Isaiah 41:10).

39. "When you pass through the waters, I will be with you; and when you pass through the rivers, they will not sweep over you. When you walk through the fire, you will not be burned; the flames will not set you ablaze. For I am the Lord your God, the Holy One of Israel, your Savior" (Isaiah 43:2–3).

40. "The Lord is good, a refuge in times of trouble. He cares for those who trust in him" (Nahum 1:7).

41. "Come to me, all you who are weary and burdened, and I will give you rest. Take my yoke upon you and

learn from me, for I am gentle and humble in heart, and you will find rest for your souls. For my yoke is easy and my burden is light" (Matthew 11:28–30).

42. "Do not let your hearts be troubled. Trust in God; trust also in me. In my Father's house are many rooms; if it were not so, I would have told you. I am going there to prepare a place for you. And if I go and prepare a place for you. I will come back and take you to be with me that you also may be where I am" (John 14:1–3).

43. "Peace I leave with you; my peace I give you. I do not give to you as the world gives. Do not let your hearts be troubled and do not be afraid" (John 14:27).

44. "We also rejoice in our sufferings, because we know that suffering produces perseverance; perseverance, character; and character, hope. And hope does not disappoint us, because God has poured out his love into our hearts by the Holy Spirit, whom he has given us" (Romans 5:3–5).

45. "The Spirit helps us in our weakness. We do not know what we ought to pray for, but the Spirit himself intercedes for us with groans that words cannot express. And he who searches our hearts knows the mind of the Spirit, because the Spirit himself intercedes for the saints in accordance with God's will" (Romans 8:26–27).

46. "In all things God works for the good of those who love him, who have been called according to his purpose" (Romans 8:28).

47. "Be joyful in hope, patient in affliction, faithful in prayer" (Romans 12:12).

48. "No temptation has seized you except what is common to man. And God is faithful; he will not let you be tempted beyond what you can bear. But when you are tempted, he will also provide a way out so that you can stand up under it" (1 Corinthians 10:13).

49. "Praise be to the God and Father of our Lord Jesus Christ, the Father of compassion and the God of all comfort, who comforts us in all our troubles, so that we can comfort those in any trouble with the comfort we ourselves have received from God" (2 Corinthians 1:3–4).

50. "We are hard pressed on every side, but not crushed; perplexed, but not in despair; persecuted, but not abandoned; struck down, but not destroyed. We always carry around in our body the death of Jesus, so that the life of Jesus may also be revealed in our body" (2 Corinthians 4:8–10).

51. "We do not lose heart. Though outwardly we are wasting away, yet inwardly we are being renewed day by day. For our light and momentary troubles are achieving for us an eternal glory that far outweighs them all. So we fix our eyes not on what is seen, but on what is unseen. For what is seen is temporary, but what is unseen is eternal" (2 Corinthians 4:16–18).

52. "He said to me, 'My grace is sufficient for you, for my power is made perfect in weakness.' Therefore I will boast all the more gladly about my weaknesses, so that Christ's power may rest on me. That is why, for Christ's sake, I delight in weaknesses, in insults, in hardships, in persecutions, in difficulties. For when I am weak, then I am strong" (2 Corinthians 12:9–10).

53. "It has been granted to you on behalf of Christ not only to believe on him, but also to suffer for him" (Philippians 1:29).

54. "I want to know Christ and the power of his resurrection and the fellowship of sharing in his sufferings, becoming like him in his death, and so, somehow, to attain to the resurrection from the dead" (Philippians 3:10–11).

55. "The Lord is faithful, and he will strengthen and protect you from the evil one. . . . May the Lord direct your hearts into God's love and Christ's perseverance" (2 Thessalonians 3:3, 5).

56. "We do not have a high priest who is unable to sympathize with our weaknesses, but we have one who has been tempted in every way, just as we are— yet was without sin. Let us then approach the throne of grace with confidence, so that we may receive mercy and find grace to help us in our time of need" (Hebrews 4:15–16).

57. "Consider it pure joy, my brothers, whenever you face trials of many kinds, because you know that the testing of your faith develops perseverance. Perseverance must finish its work so that you may be mature and complete, not lacking anything" (James 1:2–4).

58. "Blessed is the man who perseveres under trial, because when he has stood the test, he will receive the crown of life that God has promised to those who love him" (James 1:12).

59. "Dear friends, do not be surprised at the painful trial you are suffering, as though something strange were

happening you. But rejoice that you participate in the sufferings of Christ, so that you may be overjoyed when his glory is revealed" (1 Peter 4:12–13).

60. "In this you greatly rejoice, though now for a little while you may have had to suffer grief in all kinds of trials. These have come so that your faith—of greater worth than gold, which perishes even though refined by fire—may be proved genuine and may result in praise, glory and honor when Jesus Christ is revealed" (1 Peter 1:6–7).

61. "Humble yourselves, therefore, under God's mighty hand, that he may lift you up in due time. Cast all your anxiety on him because he cares for you" (1 Peter 5:6–7).

■ LIST #6
11 Women Who Were Prophets

Most prophets mentioned in the Bible were men. But ten
women were named by the Lord as prophetesses, and one
wicked woman claimed herself a prophetess.

1. Miriam

   "Miriam the prophetess, Aaron's sister, took a tambourine in her hand, and all the women followed her, with
   tambourines and dancing" (Exodus 15:20–21).

2. Deborah

   "Deborah, a prophetess, the wife of Lappidoth, was
   leading Israel at that time" (Judges 4:4).

3. Huldah

   "Hilkiah the priest, Ahikam, Acbor, Shaphan and
   Asaiah went to speak to the prophetess Huldah, who
   was the wife of Shallum son of Tikvah, the son of
   Harhas, keeper of the wardrobe" (2 Kings 22:14).

4. Noahdiah

   "Remember, my God, Tobiah and Sanballat . . . and
   also the prophetess Noahdiah . . . that would have put
   me in fear" (Nehemiah 6:14 WEB)

5. Anna

   "There was also a prophetess, Anna, the daughter of
   Phanuel, of the tribe of Asher. She was very old; she
   had lived with her husband seven years after her marriage, and then was a widow until she was eighty-four"
   (Luke 2:36–37).

6–9. Daughters of Philip

"Leaving the next day, we reached Caesarea and stayed at the house of Philip the evangelist, one of the Seven. He had four unmarried daughters who prophesied" (Acts 21:8–9).

10. Isaiah's wife

"I went to the prophetess, and she conceived and gave birth to a son. And the LORD said to me, 'Name him Maher-Shalal-Hash-Baz'" (Isaiah 8:3). [By the way, Maher-Shalal-Hash-Baz is the longest word in the entire Bible.]

11. Jezebel

"You tolerate that woman Jezebel, who calls herself a prophetess" (Revelation 2:20).

LIST #7
6 Blessings and Responsibilities for the Family

God gives many blessings, but sometimes he attaches a responsibility to that blessing.

1. Blessing
"The fruit of your womb will be blessed, and the crops of your land and the young of your livestock—the calves of your herds and the lambs of your flocks" (Deuteronomy 28:4).

Responsibility
"If you fully obey the Lord your God and carefully follow all his commands I give you today, the Lord your God will set you high above all the nations on earth. All these blessings will come upon you and accompany you if you obey the Lord your God" (Deuteronomy 28:1–2).

2. Blessing
"From everlasting to everlasting the Lord's love is with those who fear him, and his righteousness with their children's children" (Psalm 103:17).

Responsibility
"With those who keep his covenant and remember to obey his precepts" (Psalm 103:18).

3. Blessing
"Blessed are all who fear the Lord, who walk in his ways. You will eat the fruit of your labor; blessings and prosperity will be

yours. Your wife will be like a fruitful vine within your house; your sons will be like olive shoots around your table. . . . May the Lord bless you from Zion all the days of your life; may you see the prosperity of Jerusalem, and may you live to see your children's children" (Psalm 128:1–3, 5–6).

Responsibility
"Thus is the man blessed who fears the Lord" (Psalm 128:4).

4. Blessing
"The Lord watches over the alien and sustains the fatherless and the widow" (Psalm 146:9).

Responsibility
"Blessed is he whose help is the God of Jacob, whose hope is in the Lord his God, the Maker of heaven and earth, the sea, and everything in them—the Lord who remains faithful forever" (Psalm 146:5–6).

5. Blessing
"A good man leaves an inheritance for his children's children" (Proverbs 13:22).

Responsibility
One must be "good" (Proverbs 13:22).

6. Blessing
"When a child is old . . . he will not turn away from it [the way he should go]" (Proverbs 22:6).

Responsibility
"Train up a child in the way he should go" (Proverbs 22:6).

LIST #8
21 Widows

Some women in the Bible lost their husbands through natural death; others became widows through unusual or cruel circumstances. Some references to widows were only hypothetical, used to make a point—or lay a trap. Other times widows are referred to as a group.

1. The women of Shechem

   "Two of Jacob's sons, Simeon and Levi, Dinah's brothers, took their swords and attacked the unsuspecting city, killing every male" (Genesis 34:25).

2. Tamar

   "Judah got a wife for Er, his firstborn, and her name was Tamar. But Er, Judah's firstborn, was wicked in the Lord's sight; so the Lord put him to death" (Genesis 38:6–7).

3. Naomi

   "Elimelech, Naomi's husband, died, and she was left with her two sons" (Ruth 1:3).

4-5. Ruth and Orpah

   "They [Naomi's sons, Mahlon and Kilion] married Moabite women, one named Orpah and the other Ruth. After they had lived there about ten years, both Mahlon and Kilion also died, and Naomi was left without her two sons and her husband" (Ruth 1:4–5).

6. The wife of Phinehas

   "His daughter-in-law, the wife of Phinehas, was

pregnant and near the time of delivery. When she heard the news that the ark of God had been captured and that her father-in-law and her husband were dead, she went into labor and gave birth, but was overcome by her labor pains" (1 Samuel 4:19).

7. Abigail

"In the morning, when Nabal was sober, his wife told him all these things, and his heart failed him and he became like a stone. About ten days later, the LORD struck Nabal and he died" (1 Samuel 25:37–38).

8. Huram's mother

"King Solomon sent to Tyre and brought Huram, whose mother was a widow from the tribe of Naphtali and whose father was a man of Tyre and a craftsman in bronze" (1 Kings 7:13–14).

9. Jeroboam's mother

"Jeroboam son of Nebat rebelled against the king. He was one of Solomon's officials, an Ephraimite from Zeredah, and his mother was a widow named Zeruah" (1 Kings 11:26).

10. The widow at Zarephath

"Go at once to Zarephath of Sidon and stay there. I have commanded a widow in that place to supply you with food" (1 Kings 17:9).

11. Jezebel

"There was never a man like Ahab, who sold himself to do evil in the eyes of the Lord, urged on by Jezebel his wife" (1 Kings 21:25).

"Ahab rested with his fathers" (1 Kings 22:40).

12. An unnamed prophet's wife

    "The wife of a man from the company of the prophets cried out to Elisha, 'Your servant my husband is dead, and you know that he revered the Lord. But now his creditor is coming to take my two boys as his slaves'" (2 Kings 4:1).

13. The widow in the Sadducees' case study

    "The second one married the widow, but he also died, leaving no child. It was the same with the third. In fact, none of the seven left any children" (Mark 12:21–22).

14. A poor widow

    "A poor widow came and put in two very small copper coins, worth only a fraction of a penny" (Mark 12:42).

15. Anna

    "There was also a prophetess, Anna, the daughter of Phanuel, of the tribe of Asher. She was very old; she had lived with her husband seven years after her marriage, and then was a widow until she was eighty-four" (Luke 2:36–37).

16. Widows in Elijah's time

    "I assure you that there were many widows in Israel in Elijah's time" (Luke 4:25).

17. A widow from Nain

    "As he approached the town gate, a dead person was being carried out—the only son of his mother, and she was a widow" (Luke 7:12).

18. The persistent widow in Jesus's parable

    "In a certain town there was a judge who neither feared God nor cared about men. And there was a widow in that town who kept coming to him with the plea, 'Grant me justice against my adversary'" (Luke 18:2–3).

19. Sapphira

"When Ananias heard this, he fell down and died. And great fear seized all who heard what had happened. Then the young men came forward, wrapped up his body, and carried him out and buried him. About three hours later his wife came in, not knowing what had happened" (Acts 5:5–7).

20. Grecian and Hebraic Christian widows

"In those days when the number of disciples was increasing, the Grecian Jews among them complained against the Hebraic Jews because their widows were being overlooked in the daily distribution of food" (Acts 6:1).

21. Dorcas's friends

"Peter went with them, and when he arrived he was taken upstairs to the room. All the widows stood around him, crying and showing him the robes and other clothing that Dorcas had made while she was still with them" (Acts 9:39).

LIST #9
7 Scriptures on Anger

Anger is something we all have to deal with. In fact, anger is mentioned 327 times in Scripture. Here are some great insights from the Bible regarding anger.

1. "A patient man has great understanding, but a quick-tempered man displays folly" (Proverbs 14:29).

2. "A gentle answer turns away wrath, but a harsh word stirs up anger" (Proverbs 15:1).

3. "[Love] is not rude, it is not self-seeking, it is not easily angered, it keeps no record of wrongs" (1 Corinthians 13:5).

4. "'In your anger do not sin': Do not let the sun go down while you are still angry, and do not give the devil a foothold" (Ephesians 4:26–27).

5. "Get rid of all bitterness, rage and anger, brawling and slander, along with every form of malice. Be kind and compassionate to one another, forgiving each other, just as in Christ God forgave you" (Ephesians 4:31–32).

6. "Take note of this: Everyone should be quick to listen, slow to speak and slow to become angry, for man's anger does not bring about the righteous life that God desires" (James 1:19–20).

7. "The tongue also is a fire, a world of evil among the parts of the body. It corrupts the whole person, sets the whole course of his life on fire, and is itself set on fire by hell" (James 3:6).

LIST #10
4 Hairy Men

Hairy men are highlighted four times in the Bible. Perhaps the strangest instance is the story of king Nebuchadnezzar.

1. Esau

   "Jacob said to Rebekah his mother, 'But my brother Esau is a hairy man, and I'm a man with smooth skin'" (Genesis 27:11).

2. Samson

   "'No razor has ever been used on my head,' he said, 'because I have been a Nazarite set apart to God since birth'" (Judges 16:17).

3. Absalom

   "Whenever he cut the hair of his head—he used to cut his hair from time to time when it became too heavy for him—he would weigh it, and its weight was two hundred shekels by the royal standard" (2 Samuel 14:26).

4. Nebuchadnezzar

   "Immediately what had been said about Nebuchadnezzar was fulfilled. He was driven away from people and ate grass like cattle. His body was drenched with the dew of heaven until his hair grew like the feathers of an eagle and his nails like the claws of a bird" (Daniel 4:33).

■ LIST #11

26 Things the Bible Says about Sex

Sex is a gift from God, but he does warn us against misusing that gift. The Bible speaks candidly about sex in these twenty-six passages:

1. Do not commit adultery (Exodus 20:14).

2. Do not covet someone else's spouse (Exodus 20:17).

3. Do not have sex with your parent (Leviticus 18:7).

4. Do not have sex with your stepparent (Leviticus 18:8).

5. Do not have sex with your sibling or your half sibling (Leviticus 18:9, 11).

6. Do not have sex with your grandchild (Leviticus 18:10).

7. Do not have sex with your parents' siblings or their spouses (Leviticus 18:12–14).

8. Do not have sex with your children's spouses (Leviticus 18:15).

9. Do not have sex with your siblings' spouses (Leviticus 18:16).

10. Do not have sex with both a person and that person's child (Leviticus 18:17).

11. Do not have sex with both a person and that person's grandchild (Leviticus 18:17).

12. Do not have sex with two siblings (Leviticus 18:18).

13. Do not have sex with another person of the same sex (Leviticus 18:22).

14. Do not have sex with an animal (Leviticus 18:23).

15. Do not make your daughter into a prostitute (Leviticus 19:29).

16. Do not participate in cross-dressing (Deuteronomy 22:5).

17. Do not make someone drunk so you can see the person's nakedness (Habakkuk 2:15).

18. Do not lust after a person in your heart (Matthew 5:28).

19. Avoid sexual immorality (Acts 15:29).

20. Do not be involved with homosexual acts (Romans 1:26–28).

21. Sexual immorality is a sin against your own body (1 Corinthians 6:18).

22. Avoid sexual immorality; get married (1 Corinthians 7:2).

23. Husbands and wives should not deprive each other of sex (1 Corinthians 7:4–5).

24. God's will is for people to abstain from sexual immorality (1 Thessalonians 4:3–8).

25. The marriage bed is to be honored and kept pure (Hebrews 13:4).

26. Eyes filled with lust come from the world, not from God (1 John 2:16).

■ LIST #12
107 Nameless Women

The Bible lists more than one hundred instances of women who had a strong influence on their families and society, yet remain nameless. Some of them had a negative impact, but many led by their godly examples.

1. Cain's wife—Genesis 4:17

2. Seth's daughters—Genesis 5:7

3. Enosh's daughters—Genesis 5:10

4. Kenan's daughters—Genesis 5:13

5. Mahalalel's daughters—Genesis 5:16

6. Jared's daughters—Genesis 5:19

7. Enoch's daughters—Genesis 5:22

8. Methuselah's daughters—Genesis 5:26

9. Lamech's daughters—Genesis 5:30

10. Daughters of men—Genesis 6:1–4

11. Noah's wife and his sons' wives—Genesis 6:18

12. Shem's daughters, granddaughters, great-granddaughters, etc.—Genesis 11:10–26

13. Lot's wife—Genesis 19:15–26

14. Lot's daughters—Genesis 19:12–17; 30–38

15. Potiphar's wife—Genesis 39

16. Shaul's mother—Genesis 46:10

17. Pharoah's daughter—Exodus 2:5–10; Acts 7:21; Hebrews 11:24

18. Daughters of Reuel and siblings of Zipporah—Exodus 2:16–22

19. Daughters of Putiel—Exodus 6:25

20. Willing, skilled women—Exodus 35:22–29

21. Women who served at the Tent of Meeting—Exodus 38:8; 1 Samuel 2:22

22. Cushite wife of Moses—Numbers 12:1

23. Midianite women—Numbers 31:9

24. Sisera's mother—Judges 5:28–31

25. Gideon's wives and concubines—Judges 8:29–31

26. Woman of Thebez—Judges 9:50–55

27. Jephthah's mother—Judges 11:1

28. Gilead's wife—Judges 11:2–3

29. Jephthah's daughter—Judges 11:30–39

30. Ibzan's daughters—Judges 12:8–9

31. Manoah's wife—Judges 13

32. Samson's wife—Judges 14:1–20

33. Samson's sister-in-law—Judges 15:1–8

34. Micah's mother—Judges 17:1–4

35. A Levite's concubine—Judges 19:1–10, 20–30

36. Four hundred virgins of Jabesh Gilead—Judges 21

37. Women of Bethlehem—Ruth 1:19

38. Boaz's servant girls—Ruth 2:8–9

39. Daughters of Elkanah—1 Samuel 1:4; 2:21

40. Eli's daughter-in-law—1 Samuel 4:19–22

41. Girls fetching water—1 Samuel 9:11–13

42. Celebrating women of Israel—1 Samuel 18:6–7

43. Abigail's five maids—1 Samuel 25:42

44. Witch of Endor—1 Samuel 28

45. Mephibosheth's nurse—2 Samuel 4:4

46. Woman of Tekoa—2 Samuel 14:1–20

47. 10 Concubines of David—2 Samuel 15:16; 16:22; 20:3

48. Servant girl of En Rogel—2 Samuel 17:17

49. Wise woman of Abel Beth Maacah—2 Samuel 20:16–22

50. Two prostitute mothers—1 Kings 3:16–28

51. Mother of Huram—1 Kings 7:13–14; 2 Chronicles 2:13–14

52. Queen of Sheba—1 Kings 10:1–13; 2 Chronicles 9:1–12

53. Solomon's wives and concubines—1 Kings 11:1–4

54. Queen Tahpenes' sister—1 Kings 11:19–20

55. Wife of Jeroboam—1 Kings 14:1–17

56. Widow of Zarephath—1 Kings 17:8–24; Luke 4:25–26

57. Mother of Elisha—1 Kings 19:20

58. Widow of a man from the company of prophets—2 Kings 4:1–7

59. Well-to-do woman of Shunem—2 Kings 4:8–37; 8:1–6

60. Wife of Naaman—2 Kings 5:2–3

61. Maid of Naaman's wife—2 Kings 5:2–4

62. Mothers who ate their sons—2 Kings 6:26–30

63. Sheshan's daughters—1 Chronicles 2:34–35

64. Jabez's mother—1 Chronicles 4:9–10

65. Shimei's six daughters—1 Chronicles 4:27

66. Manasseh's Aramean concubine—1 Chronicles 7:14

67. Makir's wife—1 Chronicles 7:15

68. Zelophehad's daughters—1 Chronicles 7:15

69. Heman's daughters—1 Chronicles 25:5–6

70. Artaxerxes' queen—Nehemiah 2:6

71. Shallum's daughters—Nehemiah 3:12

72. Barzillai's daughter—Nehemiah 7:63

73. Foreign women—Nehemiah 13:23–27

74. Job's daughters—Job 1:4, 13, 18

75. Job's wife—Job 2:9–10

76. King Lemuel's mother—Proverbs 31:1

77. Women of Zion—Isaiah 3:16–26

78. Zedekiah's daughters—Jeremiah 41:10

79. Wicked Hebrew wives—Jeremiah 44:7–10, 15–30

80. Women who wept for the Babylonian fertility god Tammuz—Ezekiel 8:14–15

81. Ezekiel's wife—Ezekiel 24:15–18

82. Belshazzar's mother—Daniel 5:10–12

83. King of the South's daughter—Daniel 11:6–7

84. Peter's mother-in-law—Matthew 8:14–15; Mark 1:29–31; Luke 4:38–39

85. Jairus's daughter—Matthew 9:18–25; Mark 5:21–43; Luke 8:41–56

86. Woman with the issue of blood—Matthew 9:20–22; Mark 5:25–34; Luke 8:43–48

87. Jesus's sisters—Matthew 13:55–56; Mark 6:3

88. The daughter of Herodias—Matthew 14:3–12

89. Servant girls at Peter's denial—Matthew 26:69–71; Mark 14:66–69

90. Pilate's wife—Matthew 27:19

91. Women at Calvary—Matthew 27:55

92. Syrophoenician woman—Mark 7:24–30

93. Widow with two mites—Mark 12:41–44; Luke 21:1–4

94. Widow from Nain—Luke 7:11–15

95. Woman who was a sinner—Luke 7:36–50

96. A woman in the crowd who called out a blessing—Luke 11:27–28

97. Afflicted "daughter of Abraham"—Luke 13:11–16

98. Daughters of Jerusalem—Luke 23:26–28

99. Samaritan woman at the well—John 4:4–42

100. Woman caught in adultery—John 8:1–11

101. Grecian widows—Acts 6:1

102. God-fearing women of Antioch—Acts 13:50

103. Demon-possessed slave girl—Acts 16:16–19

104. Daughters of Philip—Acts 21:8–9

105. Paul's sister—Acts 23:16

106. Rufus's mother—Romans 16:13

107. Nereus's sister—Romans 16:15

LIST #13
3 Key Teachings about Adultery

The topic of adultery is mentioned fifty-two times in the Bible. Below are a few straightforward passages.

1. "You have heard that it was said, 'Do not commit adultery.' But I tell you that anyone who looks at a woman lustfully has already committed adultery with her in his heart. If your right eye causes you to sin, gouge it out and throw it away. It is better for you to lose one part of your body than for your whole body to be thrown into hell. And if your right hand causes you to sin, cut it off and throw it away. It is better for you to lose one part of your body than for your whole body to go into hell.

   "It has been said, 'Anyone who divorces his wife must give her a certificate of divorce.' But I tell you that anyone who divorces his wife, except for marital unfaithfulness, causes her to become an adulteress, and anyone who marries the divorced woman commits adultery" (Matthew 5:27–32).

2. "Anyone who divorces his wife and marries another woman commits adultery, and the man who marries a divorced woman commits adultery" (Luke 16:18).

3. "Jesus went to the Mount of Olives. At dawn he appeared again in the temple courts, where all the people gathered around him, and he sat down to teach them. The teachers of the law and the Pharisees brought in a woman caught in adultery. They made her stand before the group and said to

Jesus, 'Teacher, this woman was caught in the act of adultery. In the Law Moses commanded us to stone such women. Now what do you say?' They were using this question as a trap, in order to have a basis for accusing him.

"But Jesus bent down and started to write on the ground with his finger. When they kept on questioning him, he straightened up and said to them, 'If any one of you is without sin, let him be the first to throw a stone at her.' Again he stooped down and wrote on the ground.

"At this, those who heard began to go away one at a time, the older ones first, until only Jesus was left, with the woman still standing there. Jesus straightened up and asked her, 'Woman, where are they? Has no one condemned you?'

"'No one, sir,' she said.

"'Then neither do I condemn you,' Jesus declared. 'Go now and leave your life of sin'" (John 8:1–11).

 # LIST #14
8 Queens

Some queens in the Bible were godly, while others served idols. One wicked queen killed all of her grandchildren. Queens were mentioned in both positive and negative lights.

1. Abigail—a queen who was intelligent, beautiful, and who possessed good judgment

   - "She was an intelligent and beautiful woman" (1 Samuel 25:3).

   - "David said to Abigail, 'Praise be to the LORD, the God of Israel, who has sent you today to meet me. May you be blessed for your good judgment and for keeping me from bloodshed this day and from avenging myself with my own hands'" (1 Samuel 25:32–33).

   - "Then David sent word to Abigail, asking her to become his wife. His servants went to Carmel and said to Abigail, 'David has sent us to you to take you to become his wife'" (1 Samuel 25:39–40).

   - For more about Abigail, read 1 Samuel 25; 27:1–3; 30:1–18.

2. Athaliah—a queen who massacred her grandchildren

   - "The people of Jerusalem made Ahaziah, Jehoram's youngest son, king in his place, since the raiders, who came with the Arabs into the camp, had killed all the older sons. So Ahaziah son of Jehoram king of Judah began to reign.

"Ahaziah was twenty-two years old when he became king, and he reigned in Jerusalem one year. His mother's name was Athaliah, a granddaughter of Omri.

"He too walked in the ways of the house of Ahab, for his mother encouraged him in doing wrong" (2 Chronicles 22:1–3).

- "When Athaliah the mother of Ahaziah saw that her son was dead, she proceeded to destroy the whole royal family of the house of Judah" (2 Chronicles 22:10).

- She was called a "wicked woman" in 2 Chronicles 24:7.

- For more about Athaliah, read 2 Kings 11; 2 Chronicles 22–23.

3. Bathsheba—a queen whose first husband had been sent to his death so the king could have her

- "In the morning David wrote a letter to Joab and sent it with Uriah. In it he wrote, 'Put Uriah in the front line where the fighting is fiercest. Then withdraw from him so he will be struck down and die'" (2 Samuel 11:14).

- "When Uriah's wife heard that her husband was dead, she mourned for him. After the time of mourning was over, David had her brought to his house, and she became his wife and bore him a son. But the thing David had done displeased the LORD" (2 Samuel 11:26–27).

- For more about Bathsheba, read 2 Samuel 11–12; 1 Chronicles 3:5.

4. Esther—a queen who saved her people

- "Mordecai told him [Hathach] . . . the exact amount of money Haman had promised to pay into the royal treasury for the destruction of the Jews. He also gave him a copy of the text of the edict for their annihilation, which had been published in Susa, to show to Esther and explain it to her, and he told him to urge her to go into the king's presence to beg for mercy and plead with him for her people.

  "Hathach went back and reported to Esther what Mordecai had said. Then she instructed him to say to Mordecai, 'All the king's officials and the people of the royal provinces know that for any man or woman who approaches the king in the inner court without being summoned the king has but one law: that he be put to death. The only exception to this is for the king to extend the gold scepter to him and spare his life. But thirty days have passed since I was called to go to the king.'

  "When Esther's words were reported to Mordecai, he sent back this answer: 'Do not think that because you are in the king's house you alone of all the Jews will escape. For if you remain silent at this time, relief and deliverance for the Jews will arise from another place, but you and your father's family will perish. And who knows but that you have come to royal position for such a time as this?'

  "Then Esther sent this reply to Mordecai: 'Go, gather together all the Jews who are in Susa, and fast for me. Do not eat or drink for three days, night or day. I and my maids will fast as you do. When this is done, I will go to the king, even though it is against the law. And if I perish, I perish'" (Esther 4:7–16).

- For more about Esther, read the book of Esther.

5. Jezebel—a wicked queen

   - "He [Ahab] not only considered it trivial to commit the sins of Jeroboam son of Nebat, but he also married Jezebel daughter of Ethbaal king of the Sidonians, and began to serve Baal and worship him" (1 Kings 16:31).

   - Some scholars have suggested that the name Jezebel means "dunghill."

   - For more on Jezebel, read 1 Kings 18:4–19; 21:5–26; 2 Kings 9:30–37.

6. Maacah—a queen mother who was deposed for worshiping idols

   - "King Asa also deposed his grandmother Maacah from her position as queen mother, because she had made a repulsive Asherah pole" (2 Chronicles 15:16).

   - She was the daughter of Abishalom, the wife of King Rehoboam of Judah, and mother of Abijah (1 Kings 15:1–2).

7. Michal—a queen whose love turned to hatred

   - "Saul's daughter Michal was in love with David, and when they told Saul about it, he was pleased. 'I will give her to him,' he thought, 'so that she may be a snare to him and so that the hand of the Philistines may be against him.' So Saul said to David, 'Now you have a second opportunity to become my son-in-law'" (1 Samuel 18:20–21).

   - She was the daughter of King Saul and the wife of King David.

- For more about Michal, read 1 Samuel 18:17–30; 19:11–17; 2 Samuel 3:13–16; 6:12–23.

8. Nehushta—a queen forced into exile
   - She was the daughter of Elnathan, the wife of King Jehoiakim, and the mother of Jehoiachin (2 Kings 24:6–16; Jeremiah 13:18; 29:2).

■ LIST #15
32 Miracles Recorded in the Old Testament

A miracle is simply God introducing himself into the natural world he created and doing the unusual. This interruption of the "normal" is to get our attention. Here are just some of the miracles you can read about in the Old Testament.

1. Noah and his family were saved by entering the ark (Genesis 7:1; 8:1; 9:1–3).

2. Animals came in pairs to the ark (Genesis 7:8–9, 14–16).

3. A flood covered the whole world (Genesis 7:17–24).

4. Sarah had a baby when she was old (Genesis 18:10–14; 21:1–5).

5. God spoke to Moses from a bush that was on fire but didn't burn up (Exodus 3:2–4).

6. Aaron's staff became a snake (Exodus 7:9–10).

7. Ten plagues came upon Egypt (Exodus 7:14–12:30).

8. God went ahead of the Israelites by day in a pillar of cloud and by night in a pillar of fire to guide them (Exodus 13:21–22).

9. God parted the Red Sea (Exodus 14:21–31).

10. God provided manna in the wilderness (Exodus 16:14–35).

11. God produced water from a rock (Exodus 17:1–7).

12. Aaron's staff sprouted, budded, blossomed, and produced almonds (Numbers 17:8).

13. Looking at a bronze snake brought healing (Numbers 21:4–9).

14. The walls of Jericho fell down (Joshua 6:1–20).

15. Gideon's fleece was miraculously wet, then dry (Judges 6:36–40).

16. Elijah was fed by ravens (1 Kings 17:4–6).

17. A widow's supply of flour and oil was endless (1 Kings 17:7–16).

18. A widow's son was raised from the dead (1 Kings 17:17–24).

19. Elijah called down fire from heaven (1 Kings 18:30–39).

20. The angel fed Elijah (1 Kings 19:3–9).

21. Elijah was taken to heaven in a whirlwind (2 Kings 2:1, 11).

22. Elisha cursed young men, who were then eaten by bears (2 Kings 2:23–25).

23. Elisha miraculously provided a widow with much oil (2 Kings 4:1–7).

24. Elisha raised the Shunammite woman's son from the dead (2 Kings 4:8–37).

25. Elisha fed one hundred men with just twenty loaves of bread (2 Kings 4:42–44).

26. Naaman the leper was healed (2 Kings 5:13–14).

27. The ax head floated on the water (2 Kings 6:1–7).

28. Daniel knew and interpreted King Nebuchadnezzar's prophetic dream (Daniel 2:1–49).

29. Shadrach, Meshach, and Abednego were not burned in the fiery furnace (Daniel 3:1–30).

30. A hand wrote on the wall (Daniel 5:1–31).

31. Daniel was saved from hungry lions (Daniel 6:1–28).

32. Jonah was swallowed by a large fish (Jonah 1:15–17).

■ LIST #16
9 Principles for Dealing with Anxiety

Anxiety, worry, fear . . . all have the same root. They're all based in a lack of trust in the Lord. God is sovereign and in control, and nothing comes into our lives that he is not aware of.

1. "You have made known to me the path of life; you will fill me with joy in your presence, with eternal pleasures at your right hand" (Psalm 16:11).

2. "Do not fret because of evil men or be envious of those who do wrong; for like the grass they will soon wither, like green plants they will soon die away" (Psalm 37:1–2).

3. "Be still before the LORD and wait patiently for him; do not fret when men succeed in their ways, when they carry out their wicked schemes" (Psalm 37:7).

4. "Why are you downcast, O my soul? Why so disturbed within me? Put your hope in God, for I will yet praise him, my Savior and my God" (Psalm 43:5).

5. "When a man's ways are pleasing to the LORD, he makes even his enemies live at peace with him" (Proverbs 16:7).

6. "Do not fear, for I am with you; do not be dismayed, for I am your God. I will strengthen you and help you; I will uphold you with my righteous right hand" (Isaiah 41:10).

7. "Do not worry, saying, 'What shall we eat?' or 'What

shall we drink?' or 'What shall we wear?' For the pagans run after all these things, and your heavenly Father knows that you need them. But seek first his kingdom and his righteousness, and all these things will be given to you as well. Therefore do not worry about tomorrow, for tomorrow will worry about itself. Each day has enough trouble of its own" (Matthew 6:31–34).

8. "Do not be anxious about anything, but in everything, by prayer and petition, with thanksgiving, present your requests to God. And the peace of God, which transcends all understanding, will guard your hearts and your minds in Christ Jesus" (Philippians 4:6–7).

9. "Cast all your anxiety on him because he cares for you" (1 Peter 5:7).

■ LIST #17
22 Portraits of the Word of God

How important is the Word of God in your life? Discover some great truths about how God's Word can transform your life and your thinking.

1. "He humbled you, causing you to hunger and then feeding you with manna, which neither you nor your fathers had known, to teach you that man does not live on bread alone but on every word that comes from the mouth of the LORD" (Deuteronomy 8:3).

2. "The word is very near you; it is in your mouth and in your heart so you may obey it" (Deuteronomy 30:14).

3. "The word of the LORD is right and true" (Psalm 33:4).

4. "By the word of the LORD were the heavens made, their starry host by the breath of his mouth" (Psalm 33:6).

5. "Praise the LORD, you his angels, you mighty ones who do his bidding, who obey his word" (Psalm 103:20).

6. "He sent forth his word and healed them; he rescued them from the grave" (Psalm 107:20).

7. "How can a young man keep his way pure? By living according to your word" (Psalm 119:9).

8. "I will hasten and not delay to obey your commands" (Psalm 119:60).

9. "Your word, O LORD, is eternal; it stands firm in the heavens" (Psalm 119:89).

10. "Your word is a lamp to my feet and a light for my path" (Psalm 119:105).

11. "I will bow down toward your holy temple and will praise your name for your love and your faithfulness, for you have exalted above all things your name and your word" (Psalm 138:2).

12. "He sends his command to the earth; his word runs swiftly" (Psalm 147:15).

13. "Every word of God is flawless; he is a shield to those who take refuge in him" (Proverbs 30:5).

14. "So is my word that goes out from my mouth: It will not return to me empty, but will accomplish what I desire and achieve the purpose for which I sent it" (Isaiah 55:11).

15. "'Is not my word like fire,' declares the LORD, 'and like a hammer that breaks a rock in pieces?'" (Jeremiah 23:29).

16. "I the LORD will speak what I will, and it shall be fulfilled without delay. For in your days, you rebellious house, I will fulfill whatever I say, declares the Sovereign LORD" (Ezekiel 12:25).

17. "The Word became flesh and made his dwelling among us. We have seen his glory, the glory of the One and Only, who came from the Father, full of grace and truth" (John 1:14).

18. "Take the helmet of salvation and the sword of the Spirit, which is the word of God" (Ephesians 6:17).

19. "God's word is not chained" (2 Timothy 2:9).

20. "The word of God is living and active. Sharper than any double-edged sword, it penetrates even to dividing soul and spirit, joints and marrow; it judges the thoughts and attitudes of the heart" (Hebrews 4:12).

21. "By faith we understand that the universe was formed at God's command, so that what is seen was not made out of what was visible" (Hebrews 11:3).

22. "You have been born again, not of perishable seed, but of imperishable, through the living and enduring word of God" (1 Peter 1:23).

LIST #18

31 Passages about the Importance of Love

It has been said that love makes the world go round. The topic of love is mentioned 551 times in the Bible. Here are just a few passages about love.

1. "Let love and faithfulness never leave you; bind them around your neck, write them on the tablet of your heart" (Proverbs 3:3).

2. "May your fountain be blessed, and may you rejoice in the wife of your youth. A loving doe, a graceful deer—may her breasts satisfy you always, may you ever be captivated by her love" (Proverbs 5:18–19).

3. "Hatred stirs up dissension, but love covers over all wrongs" (Proverbs 10:12).

4. "Better a meal of vegetables where there is love than a fattened calf with hatred" (Proverbs 15:17).

5. "He who covers over an offense promotes love, but whoever repeats the matter separates close friends" (Proverbs 17:9).

6. "Love and faithfulness keep a king safe; through love his throne is made secure" (Proverbs 20:28).

7. "Better is open rebuke than hidden love" (Proverbs 27:5).

8. "[There is] a time to love and a time to hate" (Ecclesiastes 3:8).

9. "'Love the Lord your God with all your heart and with all your soul and with all your mind and with all your strength.' The second is this: 'Love your neighbor as yourself.' There is no commandment greater than these" (Mark 12:30–31).

10. "God so loved the world that he gave his one and only Son, that whoever believes in him shall not perish but have eternal life" (John 3:16).

11. "A new command I give you: Love one another. As I have loved you, so you must love one another. By this all men will know that you are my disciples, if you love one another" (John 13:34–35).

12. "If you love me, you will obey what I command" (John 14:15).

13. "My command is this: Love each other as I have loved you. Greater love has no one than this, that he lay down his life for his friends. You are my friends if you do what I command. I no longer call you servants, because a servant does not know his master's business. Instead, I have called you friends, for everything that I learned from my Father I have made known to you. You did not choose me, but I chose you and appointed you to go and bear fruit—fruit that will last. Then the Father will give you whatever you ask in my name. This is my command: Love each other" (John 15:12–17).

14. "Love must be sincere. Hate what is evil; cling to what is good. Be devoted to one another in brotherly love. Honor one another above yourselves" (Romans 12:9–10).

15. "Let no debt remain outstanding, except the continuing debt to love one another; for he who loves his fellowman has fulfilled the law" (Romans 13:8).

16. "Knowledge puffs up, but love builds up" (1 Corinthians 8:1).

17. "Love is patient, love is kind. It does not envy, it does not boast, it is not proud. It is not rude, it is not self-seeking, it is not easily angered, it keeps no record of wrongs. Love does not delight in evil but rejoices with the truth. It always protects, always trusts, always hopes, always perseveres. Love never fails" (1 Corinthians 13:4–8).

18. "And now these three remain: faith, hope and love. But the greatest of these is love" (1 Corinthians 13:13).

19. "You, my brothers, were called to be free. But do not use your freedom to indulge the sinful nature; rather, serve one another in love. The entire law is summed up in a single command: 'Love your neighbor as yourself'" (Galatians 5:13–14).

20. "The fruit of the Spirit is love, joy, peace, patience, kindness, goodness, faithfulness, gentleness and self-control. Against such things there is no law" (Galatians 5:22–23).

21. "Be completely humble and gentle; be patient, bearing with one another in love" (Ephesians 4:2).

22. "Husbands, love your wives, just as Christ loved the church and gave himself up for her" (Ephesians 5:25).

23. "Husbands, love your wives and do not be harsh with them" (Colossians 3:19).

24. "Now about brotherly love we do not need to write to you, for you yourselves have been taught by God to love each other" (1 Thessalonians 4:9).

25. "Pursue righteousness, godliness, faith, love, endurance and gentleness" (1 Timothy 6:11).

26. "God did not give us a spirit of timidity, but a spirit of power, of love and of self-discipline" (2 Timothy 1:7).

27. "If you really keep the royal law found in Scripture, 'Love your neighbor as yourself,' you are doing right" (James 2:8).

28. "Above all, love each other deeply, because love covers over a multitude of sins" (1 Peter 4:8).

29. "This is how we know what love is: Jesus Christ laid down his life for us. And we ought to lay down our lives for our brothers. If anyone has material possessions and sees his brother in need but has no pity on him, how can the love of God be in him? Dear children, let us not love with words or tongue but with actions and in truth" (1 John 3:16–18).

30. "Dear friends, let us love one another, for love comes from God. Everyone who loves has been born of God and knows God. Whoever does not love does not know God, because God is love. This is how God showed his love among us: He sent his one and only Son into the world that we might live through him. This is love: not that we loved God, but that he loved us and sent his Son as an atoning sacrifice for our sins. Dear friends, since God so loved us, we also ought to love one another. No one has ever seen God; but if we love one another, God lives in us and his love is made complete in us" (1 John 4:7–12).

31. "God is love. Whoever lives in love lives in God, and God in him. In this way, love is made complete among us so that we will have confidence on the day of judgment, because in this world we are like him. There is no fear in love. But perfect love drives out fear, because fear has to do with punishment. The one who fears is not made perfect in love.

    "We love because he first loved us. If anyone says, 'I love God,' yet hates his brother, he is a liar. For anyone who does not love his brother, whom he has seen, cannot love God, whom he has not seen. And he has given us this command: Whoever loves God must also love his brother" (1 John 4:16–21).

◼ LIST #19
5 Tips for Dealing with Disagreements

One doesn't have to live long to discover that relationships aren't always harmonious. Disagreement occurs in the home, in the workplace, and even in the church. But the Bible gives us some pointers on how to handle these disruptions.

1. "If you are offering your gift at the altar and there remember that your brother has something against you, leave your gift there in front of the altar. First go and be reconciled to your brother; then come and offer your gift.

   "Settle matters quickly with your adversary who is taking you to court. Do it while you are still with him on the way, or he may hand you over to the judge, and the judge may hand you over to the officer, and you may be thrown into prison" (Matthew 5:23–25).

2. "If your brother sins against you, go and show him his fault, just between the two of you. If he listens to you, you have won your brother over. But if he will not listen, take one or two others along, so that 'every matter may be established by the testimony of two or three witnesses'" (Matthew 18:15–16).

3. "I urge you, brothers, to watch out for those who cause divisions and put obstacles in your way that are contrary to the teaching you have learned. Keep away from them" (Romans 16:17).

4. "I appeal to you, brothers, in the name of our Lord Jesus Christ, that all of you agree with one another

so that there may be no divisions among you and that you may be perfectly united in mind and thought" (1 Corinthians 1:10).

5. "Get rid of all bitterness, rage and anger, brawling and slander, along with every form of malice. Be kind and compassionate to one another, forgiving each other, just as in Christ God forgave you" (Ephesians 4:31–32).

LIST #20
6 Gentile Queens

One queen committed adultery, one defied her husband, and another was on a search for wisdom. Only a few non-Jewish queens are mentioned in Scripture.

1. Bernice—a queen who had questionable passions

   - "King Agrippa and Bernice arrived at Caesarea to pay their respects to Festus" (Acts 25:13).

   - Bernice was the companion of King Agrippa II. Secular history suggests that she was the eldest daughter of Herod Agrippa I and was married to her uncle, the king of Chalcis. Vespasian was attracted to her, as was his son Titus, who took her as his mistress and almost married her. Public opinion mounted against her becoming queen, and Titus was forced to dismiss her. See Acts 25:13, 23; 26:30.

2. Candace—a queen from Ethiopia

   - "[Philip] met an Ethiopian eunuch, an important official in charge of all the treasury of Candace, queen of the Ethiopians" (Acts 8:27).

   - Candace was queen over the Ethiopian eunuch whom Philip the evangelist baptized. See Acts 8:27–39.

3. Herodias—a queen who committed adultery

   - "Herod had arrested John and bound him and put him in prison because of Herodias, his brother Philip's wife, for John had been saying to him: 'It is not lawful for you to have her'" (Matthew 14:3–4).

- Herodias left her first husband and became the wife of Herod Antipas. Some refer to her as the Jezebel of the New Testament. See Matthew 14:1–12; Mark 6:17–29.

4. The Queen of Sheba—a queen on a search

- "When the queen of Sheba heard about the fame of Solomon and his relation to the name of the LORD, she came to test him with hard questions" (1 Kings 10:1–2).

- The Queen of Sheba was also referred to as the Queen of the South. Jewish historian Josephus suggested that her name was Nikauli. See 1 Kings 10:1–13; 2 Chronicles 9:1–12; Matthew 12:42.

5. Tahpenes—a queen who was Pharaoh's wife

- "Pharaoh was so pleased with Hadad that he gave him a sister of his own wife, Queen Tahpenes, in marriage" (1 Kings 11:19).

6. Vashti—a queen who refused the request of King Xerxes

- "On the seventh day, when King Xerxes was in high spirits from wine, he commanded the seven eunuchs who served him . . . to bring before him Queen Vashti, wearing her royal crown, in order to display her beauty to the people and nobles, for she was lovely to look at" (Esther 1:10–11).

- Vashti preceded Queen Esther on the throne of Persia. See Esther 1–2.

LIST #21

7 Instances of People Who Were Struck Blind or Speechless

On various occasions God has chosen to strike people with blindness or has caused them to be unable to speak. Eighty-six times the words *blind* or *blindness* are used in the New International Version of the Bible. Fifteen times the words *mute* or *dumb* (unable to speak) are used. Without question, these two maladies got the attention of the people involved.

People Who Were Struck Blind

1. The men of Sodom were struck blind by angels who came to rescue Lot and his family (Genesis 19:11).

2. The Lord warned that he would afflict the disobedient with diseases, fevers, plagues, defeats before their enemies, tumors, madness, blindness, and other afflictions (Deuteronomy 28:20–28).

3. When the Syrian army came to capture Elisha, he asked God to strike the army with blindness (2 Kings 6:18).

4. After Saul's encounter with the Lord on the road to Damascus, he was struck blind for three days (Acts 9:1–9).

5. The sorcerer named Elymas was struck blind at the word of the apostle Paul because he was attempting to turn Sergius Paulus away from the faith (Acts 13:6–12).

People Who Were Struck Dumb

1. The Lord caused Ezekiel's tongue to stick to the roof of his mouth so he couldn't speak (Ezekiel 3:25–27).

2. The angel Gabriel caused Zechariah to be struck dumb and unable to talk until his son was born (Luke 1:5–22, 62–66).

◼ LIST #22
6 Friendship Proverbs

The concept of friends and friendship is mentioned 125 times in the Bible. Here are a few "friendly" proverbs.

1. "A friend loves at all times, and a brother is born for adversity" (Proverbs 17:17).

2. "A man of many companions may come to ruin, but there is a friend who sticks closer than a brother" (Proverbs 18:24).

3. "Wounds from a friend can be trusted, but an enemy multiplies kisses" (Proverbs 27:6).

4. "Perfume and incense bring joy to the heart, and the pleasantness of one's friend springs from his earnest counsel. Do not forsake your friend and the friend of your father" (Proverbs 27:9–10).

5. "As iron sharpens iron, so one man sharpens another" (Proverbs 27:17).

6. "If one falls down, his friend can help him up. But pity the man who falls and has no one to help him up" (Ecclesiastes 4:10).

■ LIST #23
64 Bible Promises for Happiness

In the Bible, the word sometimes translated "blessed" can also be translated "happy." If you would like to know happiness, consider some of the Bible's suggestions on how to find this wonderful blessing.

1. "Blessed [happy] is the man whom God corrects; so do not despise the discipline of the Almighty" (Job 5:17).

2. "Blessed [happy] is the man who does not walk in the counsel of the wicked or stand in the way of sinners or sit in the seat of mockers. But his delight is in the law of the LORD, and on his law he meditates day and night. He is like a tree planted by streams of water, which yields its fruit in season and whose leaf does not wither. Whatever he does prospers" (Psalm 1:1–3).

3. "Blessed [happy] are all who take refuge in him" (Psalm 2:12).

4. "Blessed [happy] is he whose transgressions are forgiven, whose sins are covered" (Psalm 32:1).

5. "Blessed [happy] is the man whose sin the LORD does not count against him and in whose spirit is no deceit" (Psalm 32:2).

6. "Taste and see that the LORD is good; blessed [happy] is the man who takes refuge in him" (Psalm 34:8).

7. "Blessed [happy] is the man who makes the LORD his trust, who does not look to the proud, to those who turn aside to false gods" (Psalm 40:4).

8. "Blessed [happy] is he who has regard for the weak; the LORD delivers him in times of trouble. The LORD will protect him and preserve his life; he will bless him in the land and not surrender him to the desire of his foes. The LORD will sustain him on his sickbed and restore him from his bed of illness" (Psalm 41:1–3).

9. "Blessed [happy] are those you choose and bring near to live in your courts! We are filled with the good things of your house, of your holy temple. You answer us with awesome deeds of righteousness, O God our Savior, the hope of all the ends of the earth and of the farthest seas" (Psalm 65:4–5).

10. "Blessed [happy] are those who dwell in your house; they are ever praising you" (Psalm 84:4).

11. "Blessed [happy] are those whose strength is in you" (Psalm 84:5).

12. "O LORD Almighty, blessed [happy] is the man who trusts in you" (Psalm 84:12).

13. "Blessed [happy] are those who have learned to acclaim you, who walk in the light of your presence, O LORD. They rejoice in your name all day long; they exult in your righteousness. For you are their glory and strength, and by your favor you exalt our horn" (Psalm 89:15–17).

14. "Blessed [happy] is the man you discipline, O LORD, the man you teach from your law; you grant him relief from days of trouble, till a pit is dug for the wicked" (Psalm 94:12–13).

15. "Blessed [happy] are they who maintain justice, who constantly do what is right" (Psalm 106:3).

16. "Blessed [happy] is the man who fears the LORD, who finds great delight in his commands" (Psalm 112:1).

17. "Blessed [happy] is he who comes in the name of the LORD" (Psalm 118:26).

18. "Blessed [happy] are they whose ways are blameless, who walk according to the law of the LORD. Blessed are they who keep his statutes and seek him with all their heart" (Psalm 119:1–2).

19. "Sons are a heritage from the LORD, children a reward from him. Like arrows in the hands of a warrior are sons born in one's youth. Blessed [happy] is the man whose quiver is full of them" (Psalm 127:3–5).

20. "Blessed [happy] are all who fear the LORD, who walk in his ways. You will eat the fruit of your labor; blessings and prosperity will be yours. Your wife will be like a fruitful vine within your house; your sons will be like olive shoots around your table. Thus is the man blessed who fears the LORD" (Psalm 128:1–4).

21. "Blessed [happy] are the people whose God is the LORD" (Psalm 144:15).

22. "Blessed [happy] is he whose help is the God of Jacob, whose hope is in the LORD his God, the Maker of heaven and earth, the sea, and everything in them—the LORD, who remains faithful forever. He upholds the cause of the oppressed and gives food to the hungry. The LORD sets prisoners free, the LORD gives sight to the blind" (Psalm 146:5–8).

23. "Blessed [happy] is the man who finds wisdom, the man who gains understanding, for she is more profitable than silver and yields better returns than

gold. She is more precious than rubies; nothing you desire can compare with her. Long life is in her right hand; in her left hand are riches and honor. Her ways are pleasant ways, and all her paths are peace" (Proverbs 3:13–17).

24. "May your fountain be blessed [happy], and may you rejoice in the wife of your youth. A loving doe, a graceful deer—may her breasts satisfy you always, may you ever be captivated by her love" (Proverbs 5:18–19).

25. "Now then, my sons, listen to me; blessed [happy] are those who keep my ways. Listen to my instruction and be wise; do not ignore it" (Proverbs 8:32–33).

26. "Blessed [happy] is the man who listens to me, watching daily at my gates, waiting at my doorposts. For he who finds me finds life and obtains favor from the LORD" (Proverbs 8:34–35 NASB).

27. "He who despises his neighbor sins, but happy is he who is gracious to the poor" (Proverbs 14:21 NASB).

28. "He who gives attention to the word will find good, and blessed is he who trusts in the LORD" (Proverbs 16:20 NASB).

29. "A righteous man who walks in his integrity—how blessed are his sons after him" (Proverbs 20:7 NASB).

30. "He who is generous will be blessed, for he gives some of his food to the poor" (Proverbs 22:9 NASB).

31. "How blessed [happy] is the man who fears always, but he who hardens his heart will fall into calamity" (Proverbs 28:14 NASB).

32. "A faithful man will abound with blessings, but he who makes haste to be rich will not go unpunished" (Proverbs 28:20 NASB).

33. "Where there is no vision, the people are unrestrained, but happy is he who keeps the law" (Proverbs 29:18 NASB).

34. "Therefore the LORD longs to be gracious to you, and therefore He waits on high to have compassion on you for the LORD is a God of justice; how blessed are all those who long for Him" (Isaiah 30:18 NASB).

35. "Blessed is the man who trusts in the LORD and whose trust is the LORD. For he will be like a tree planted by the water, that extends its roots by a stream and will not fear when the heat comes; but its leaves will be green, and it will not be anxious in a year of drought nor cease to yield fruit" (Jeremiah 17:7–8 NASB).

36. "Blessed are the poor in spirit, for theirs is the kingdom of heaven" (Matthew 5:3 NASB).

37. "Blessed are those who mourn, for they shall be comforted" (Matthew 5:4 NASB).

38. "Blessed are the gentle, for they shall inherit the earth" (Matthew 5:5 NASB).

39. "Blessed are those who hunger and thirst for righteousness, for they shall be satisfied" (Matthew 5:6 NASB).

40. "Blessed are the merciful, for they shall receive mercy" (Matthew 5:7 NASB).

41. "Blessed are the pure in heart, for they shall see God" (Matthew 5:8 NASB).

42. "Blessed are the peacemakers, for they shall be called sons of God" (Matthew 5:9 NASB).

43. "Blessed are those who have been persecuted for the sake of righteousness, for theirs is the kingdom of heaven" (Matthew 5:10 NASB).

44. "Blessed are you when people insult you and persecute you, and falsely say all kinds of evil against you because of Me" (Matthew 5:11 NASB).

45. "The crowds going ahead of Him, and those who followed, were shouting, 'Hosanna to the Son of David; blessed is he who comes in the name of the LORD; Hosanna in the highest!'" (Matthew 21:9 NASB).

46. "But He said, 'On the contrary, blessed are those who hear the word of God and observe it'" (Luke 11:28 NASB).

47. "When one of those who were reclining at the table with Him heard this, he said to Him, 'Blessed is everyone who will eat bread in the kingdom of God!'" (Luke 14:15 NASB).

48. "So when He had washed their feet, and taken His garments and reclined at the table again, He said to them, 'Do you know what I have done to you?
    "'You call Me Teacher and Lord; and you are right, for so I am. If I then, the Lord and the Teacher, washed your feet, you also ought to wash one another's feet. For I gave you an example that you also should do as I did to you. Truly, truly, I say to you,

a slave is not greater than his master, nor is one who is sent greater than the one who sent him. If you know these things, you are blessed if you do them'" (John 13:12–17 NASB).

49. "Jesus said to him, 'Because you have seen Me, have you believed? Blessed are they who did not see, and yet believed'" (John 20:29 NASB).

50. "In everything I showed you that by working hard in this manner you must help the weak and remember the words of the Lord Jesus, that He Himself said, 'It is more blessed to give than to receive'" (Acts 20:35 NASB).

51. "Blessed [happy] are they whose transgressions are forgiven, whose sins are covered" (Romans 4:7).

52. "Blessed are those whose lawless deeds have been forgiven, and those sins have been covered" (Romans 4:8 NASB).

53. "The faith which you have, have as your own conviction before God. Happy is he who does not condemn himself in what he approves. But he who doubts is condemned if he eats, because his eating is not from faith; and whatever is not from faith is sin" (Romans 14:22–23 NASB).

54. "For the grace of God has appeared, bringing salvation to all men, instructing us to deny ungodliness and worldly desires and to live sensibly, righteously and godly in the present age, looking for the blessed hope and the appearing of the glory of our great God and Savior, Christ Jesus, who gave Himself for us to redeem us from every lawless deed, and to purify for Himself a people for His own

possession, zealous for good deeds" (Titus 2:11–14 NASB).

55. "Blessed is a man who perseveres under trial; for once he has been approved, he will receive the crown of life which the Lord has promised to those who love Him" (James 1:12 NASB).

56. "But one who looks intently at the perfect law, the law of liberty, and abides by it, not having become a forgetful hearer but an effectual doer, this man will be blessed in what he does" (James 1:25 NASB).

57. "Who is there to harm you if you prove zealous for what is good? But even if you should suffer for the sake of righteousness, you are blessed and do not fear their intimidation, and do not be troubled, but sanctify Christ as Lord in your hearts, always being ready to make a defense to everyone who asks you to give an account for the hope that is in you, yet with gentleness and reverence; and keep a good conscience so that in the thing in which you are slandered, those who revile your good behavior in Christ will be put to shame. For it is better, if God should will it so, that you suffer for doing what is right rather than for doing what is wrong" (1 Peter 3:13–17 NASB).

58. "If you are reviled for the name of Christ, you are blessed, because the Spirit of glory and of God rests on you" (1 Peter 4:14 NASB).

59. "Blessed is he who reads and those who hear the words of the prophecy, and heed the things which are written in it; for the time is near" (Revelation 1:3 NASB).

60. "Behold, I am coming like a thief. Blessed is the one who stays awake and keeps his clothes, so that he will not walk about naked and men will not see his shame" (Revelation 16:15 NASB).

61. "Then he said to me, 'Write, "Blessed are those who are invited to the marriage supper of the Lamb."' And he said to me, 'These are true words of God'" (Revelation 19:9 NASB).

62. "Blessed and holy is the one who has a part in the first resurrection; over these the second death has no power, but they will be priests of God and of Christ and will reign with Him for a thousand years" (Revelation 20:6 NASB).

63. "And behold, I am coming quickly. Blessed is he who heeds the words of the prophecy of this book" (Revelation 22:7 NASB).

64. "Blessed are those who wash their robes, so that they may have the right to the tree of life, and may enter by the gates into the city" (Revelation 22:14 NASB).

LIST #24
8 Keys for Overcoming Discouragement

No one likes to be discouraged. Discouragement is a difficult emotion to deal with, but the Bible offers some suggestions for those who are downcast.

1. "Have I not commanded you? Be strong and courageous! Do not tremble or be dismayed, for the LORD your God is with you wherever you go" (Joshua 1:9 NASB).

2. "Wait for the LORD; Be strong and let your heart take courage; Yes, wait for the LORD" (Psalm 27:14 NASB).

3. "Why are you in despair, O my soul? And why are you disturbed within me? Hope in God, for I shall again praise Him, the help of my countenance and my God" (Psalm 43:5 NASB).

4. "Do not let your heart be troubled; believe in God, believe also in Me. In My Father's house are many dwelling places; if it were not so, I would have told you; for I go to prepare a place for you. If I go and prepare a place for you, I will come again and receive you to Myself, that where I am, there you may be also" (John 14:1–3 NASB).

5. "Peace I leave with you; My peace I give to you; not as the world gives do I give to you. Do not let your heart be troubled, nor let it be fearful" (John 14:27 NASB).

6. "Therefore let us draw near with confidence to the throne of grace, so that we may receive mercy and find grace to help in time of need" (Hebrews 4:16 NASB).

7. "In this you greatly rejoice, even though now for a little while, if necessary, you have been distressed by various trials, so that the proof of your faith, being more precious than gold which is perishable, even though tested by fire, may be found to result in praise and glory and honor at the revelation of Jesus Christ" (1 Peter 1:6–7 NASB).

8. "This is the confidence which we have before Him, that, if we ask anything according to His will, He hears us. And if we know that He hears us in whatever we ask, we know that we have the requests which we have asked from Him" (1 John 5:14–15 NASB).

LIST #25
23 Important Women

Scripture indicates that particular women had great influence. Sarah, Rachel, and Esther top the list. Other women like Rebekah, Leah, Naomi, and Ruth are also mentioned. Their lives would be worthy of study.

1. Sarai / Sarah—mentioned 53 times in the Bible

2. Rachel—mentioned 46 times in the Bible

3. Esther—mentioned 44 times in the Bible

4. Leah—mentioned 32 times in the Bible

5. Rebekah—mentioned 32 times in the Bible

6. Naomi—mentioned 26 times in the Bible

7. Mary (mother of Jesus)—mentioned 22 times in the Bible

8. Ruth—mentioned 21 times in the Bible

9. Abigail—mentioned 17 times in the Bible

10. Jezebel—mentioned 17 times in the Bible

11. Michal—mentioned 17 times in the Bible

12. Hagar—mentioned 15 times in the Bible

13. Rahab—mentioned 13 times in the Bible

14. Hannah—mentioned 12 times in the Bible

15. Mary Magdalene—mentioned 12 times in the Bible

16. Miriam—mentioned 12 times in the Bible

17. Bathsheba—mentioned 11 times in the Bible

18. Martha—mentioned 11 times in the Bible

19. Vashti—mentioned 10 times in the Bible

20. Elizabeth—mentioned 10 times in the Bible

21. Queen of Sheba—mentioned 8 times in the Bible

22. Delilah—mentioned 7 times in the Bible

23. Lydia—mentioned 2 times in the Bible

■ LIST #26
10 People Who Came Back to Life

Has anyone ever "cheated" death? The answer is yes. At least ten people have.

1. The son of the widow of Zarephath was raised from the dead by Elijah (1 Kings 17:17–24).

2. The son of the Shunammite woman was raised from the dead by Elisha (2 Kings 4:32–37).

3. The man whose body touched the dead bones of Elisha came back to life (2 Kings 13:20–21).

4. The son of the widow of Nain was raised from the dead by Jesus (Luke 7:11–15).

5. Jesus rose from the dead (Matthew 28:1–10; Mark 16:1–6; Luke 24:1–7).

6. Many people rose from the dead at the time of Jesus's resurrection (Matthew 27:50–53).

7. The daughter of Jairus was raised from the dead by Jesus (Luke 8:41–42, 49–55).

8. Lazarus was raised from the dead by Jesus (John 11:1–44).

9. Dorcas was raised from the dead by Peter (Acts 9:36–41).

10. Eutychus was raised from the dead by the apostle Paul (Acts 20:9–12).

■ LIST #27
12 Things to Remember When Facing Fear

Fear can be debilitating. It drains our energy and gets us to focus on problems rather than the Problem Solver. Here are twelve passages from the Bible about fear.

1. "The LORD is my light and my salvation; whom shall I fear? The LORD is the defense of my life; whom shall I dread?" (Psalm 27:1 NASB).

2. "In God I have put my trust, I shall not be afraid. What can man do to me?" (Psalm 56:11 NASB).

3. "For you have made the LORD, my refuge, even the Most High, your dwelling place. No evil will befall you, nor will any plague come near your tent" (Psalm 91:9–10 NASB).

4. "I will lift up my eyes to the mountains; from where shall my help come? My help comes from the LORD, Who made heaven and earth" (Psalm 121:1–2 NASB).

5. "The LORD will protect you from all evil; He will keep your soul. The LORD will guard your going out and your coming in from this time forth and forever" (Psalm 121:7–8 NASB).

6. "Do not be afraid of sudden fear nor of the onslaught of the wicked when it comes; for the LORD will be your confidence and will keep your foot from being caught" (Proverbs 3:25–26 NASB).

7. "The fear of man brings a snare, but he who trusts in the LORD will be exalted" (Proverbs 29:25 NASB).

8. "For I am convinced that neither death, nor life, nor angels, nor principalities, nor things present, nor things to come, nor powers, nor height, nor depth, nor any other created thing, will be able to separate us from the love of God, which is in Christ Jesus our Lord" (Romans 8:37–39 NASB).

9. "Finally, brethren, whatever is true, whatever is honorable, whatever is right, whatever is pure, whatever is lovely, whatever is of good repute, if there is any excellence and if anything worthy of praise, dwell on these things. The things you have learned and received and heard and seen in me, practice these things, and the God of peace will be with you" (Philippians 4:8–9 NASB).

10. "For God has not given us a spirit of timidity, but of power and love and discipline" (2 Timothy 1:7 NASB).

11. "There is no fear in love; but perfect love casts out fear, because fear involves punishment, and the one who fears is not perfected in love" (1 John 4:18 NASB).

12. "Now to Him who is able to keep you from stumbling, and to make you stand in the presence of His glory blameless with great joy, to the only God our Savior, through Jesus Christ our Lord, be glory, majesty, dominion and authority, before all time and now and forever. Amen" (Jude 24–25 NASB).

■ LIST #28
28 Observations about Angels

The Bible mentions angels (including evil angels, or demons) 299 times. These created beings have great knowledge and power. They have had an amazing influence in the lives of people throughout history.

1. Children seem to have personal angels.
   - "See that you do not despise one of these little ones, for I say to you that their angels in heaven continually see the face of My Father who is in heaven" (Matthew 18:10 NASB).

2. Angels do not marry.
   - "For in the resurrection they neither marry nor are given in marriage, but are like angels in heaven" (Matthew 22:30 NASB).

3. Angels rejoice when someone repents.
   - "In the same way, I tell you, there is joy in the presence of the angels of God over one sinner who repents" (Luke 15:10 NASB).

4. Angels are God's servants.
   - "And of the angels He says, 'Who makes his angels winds, and his ministers a flame of fire'" (Hebrews 1:7 NASB).

5. A great number of angels or demons can be in a limited space.
   - "And Jesus asked him, 'What is your name?' And he said, 'Legion'; for many demons had entered him.

They were imploring Him not to command them to go away into the abyss" (Luke 8:30–31 NASB).

6. Fallen angels seek rest but do not find it.

- "Now when the unclean spirit goes out of a man, it passes through waterless places seeking rest, and does not find it" (Matthew 12:43 NASB).

7. Angels have great wisdom.

- "In order to change the appearance of things your servant Joab has done this thing. But my lord is wise, like the wisdom of the angel of God, to know all that is in the earth" (2 Samuel 14:20 NASB).

8. Angels have great power.

- "Bless the LORD, you His angels, mighty in strength, who perform His word, obeying the voice of His word!" (Psalm 103:20 NASB).

- "And behold, a severe earthquake had occurred, for an angel of the Lord descended from heaven and came and rolled away the stone and sat upon it. And his appearance was like lightning, and his clothing as white as snow. The guards shook for fear of him and became like dead men" (Matthew 28:2–4 NASB).

- ". . . and especially those who indulge the flesh in its corrupt desires and despise authority. Daring, self-willed, they do not tremble when they revile angelic majesties, whereas angels who are greater in might and power do not bring a reviling judgment against them before the Lord" (2 Peter 2:10–11 NASB).

- "But during the night an angel of the Lord opened the gates of the prison, and taking them out he said, 'Go, stand and speak to the people in the temple the whole message of this life'" (Acts 5:19–20 NASB).

- "And behold, an angel of the Lord suddenly appeared and a light shone in the cell; and he struck Peter's side and woke him up, saying, 'Get up quickly.' And his chains fell off his hands" (Acts 12:7 NASB).

- "And immediately an angel of the Lord struck him because he did not give God the glory, and he was eaten by worms and died" (Acts 12:23 NASB).

9. Angels have been revealed in bodily form.

- Angels appeared to Lot in the city of Sodom (Genesis 19).

- "Then the angel of the LORD came and sat under the oak that was in Ophrah, which belonged to Joash the Abiezrite as his son Gideon was beating out wheat in the wine press in order to save it from the Midianites. The angel of the LORD appeared to him and said to him, 'The LORD is with you, O valiant warrior'" (Judges 6:11–12 NASB).

- "Do not neglect to show hospitality to strangers, for by this some have entertained angels without knowing it" (Hebrews 13:2 NASB).

10. There are great numbers of angels.

- "A river of fire was flowing and coming out from before Him; thousands upon thousands were attending Him, and myriads upon myriads were standing before Him; the court sat, and the books were opened" (Daniel 7:10 NASB).

- "Then I looked, and I heard the voice of many angels around the throne and the living creatures and the elders; and the number of them was myriads of myriads, and thousands of thousands, saying with a loud voice, 'Worthy is the Lamb that was slain to receive power and riches and wisdom and might and honor and glory and blessing'" (Revelation 5:11–12 NASB).

11. Angels have organization and hierarchy.

- "Micaiah said, 'Therefore, hear the word of the LORD. I saw the LORD sitting on His throne, and all the host of heaven standing by Him on His right and on His left'" (1 Kings 22:19 NASB).

- "Or do you think that I cannot appeal to my Father, and He will at once put at my disposal more than twelve legions of angels?" (Matthew 26:53 NASB).

- "You followed the ways of this world and of the ruler of the kingdom of the air" (Ephesians 2:2).

- "Put on the full armor of God, so that you will be able to stand firm against the schemes of the devil. For our struggle is not against flesh and blood, but against the rulers, against the powers, against the world forces of this darkness, against the spiritual forces of wickedness in the heavenly places" (Ephesians 6:11–12 NASB).

- "I know where you dwell, where Satan's throne is; and you hold fast My name, and did not deny My faith even in the days of Antipas, My witness, My faithful one, who was killed among you, where Satan dwells" (Revelation 2:13 NASB).

- "And the armies which are in heaven, clothed in fine linen, white and clean, were following Him on white horses" (Revelation 19:14 NASB).

12. Angels are not to be worshiped.

   "Let no one keep defrauding you of your prize by delighting in self-abasement and the worship of the angels, taking his stand on visions he has seen, inflated without cause by his fleshly mind" (Colossians 2:18 NASB).

13. Cherubim chiefly serve as guardians of the throne of God.

   - "The cherubim shall have their wings spread upward, covering the mercy seat with their wings and facing one another; the faces of the cherubim are to be turned toward the mercy seat. You shall put the mercy seat on top of the ark, and in the ark you shall put the testimony which I will give to you. There I will meet with you; and from above the mercy seat, from between the two cherubim which are upon the ark of the testimony, I will speak to you about all that I will give you in commandment for the sons of Israel" (Exodus 25:20–22 NASB).

   - "It came about when He commanded the man clothed in linen, saying, 'Take fire from between the whirling wheels, from between the cherubim,' he entered and stood beside a wheel. Then the cherub stretched out his hand from between the cherubim to the fire which was between the cherubim, took some and put it into the hands of the one clothed in linen, who took it and went out. The cherubim appeared to have the form of a man's hand under their wings. Then I looked, and behold, four wheels beside the cherubim, one wheel beside each cherub; and the appearance of the wheels was like the gleam of a Tarshish stone. As for their appearance, all four of them had the same likeness, as if one wheel were within another wheel. When they moved, they went in any of their four directions without turning as they went; but they followed in the direction which they faced, without turning as they went. Their whole body, their backs, their hands, their wings and the wheels were full of eyes all around, the wheels belonging to all four of them. The wheels were called in my hearing, the whirling wheels. And each one had four faces. The first face was the face of a cherub, the second face was the face of a man, the third the face of a lion, and the fourth the face of an eagle. Then the cherubim rose up. They are the living beings that I saw by the river Chebar.

"Now when the cherubim moved, the wheels would go beside them; also when the cherubim lifted up their wings to rise from the ground, the wheels would not turn from beside them. When the cherubim stood still, the wheels would stand still; and when they rose up, the wheels would rise with them, for the spirit of the living beings was in them" (Ezekiel 10:6–17 NASB).

- ". . . over the entrance, and to the inner house, and on the outside, and on all the wall all around inside and outside, by measurement. It was carved with cherubim and palm trees; and a palm tree was between cherub and cherub, and every cherub had two faces, a man's face toward the palm tree on one side and a young lion's face toward the palm tree on the other side; they were carved on all the house all around" (Ezekiel 41:17–19 NASB).

- "And before the throne there was something like a sea of glass, like crystal; and in the center and around the throne, four living creatures full of eyes in front and behind. The first creature was like a lion, and the second creature like a calf, and the third creature had a face like that of a man, and the fourth creature was like a flying eagle. And the four living creatures, each one of them having six wings, are full of eyes around and within; and day and night they do not cease to say, 'HOLY, HOLY, HOLY IS THE LORD GOD, THE ALMIGHTY, WHO WAS AND WHO IS AND WHO IS TO COME.' And when the living creatures give glory and honor and thanks to Him who sits on the throne, to Him who lives forever and ever, the twenty-four elders will fall down before Him who sits on the throne, and will worship Him who lives forever and ever" (Revelation 4:6–10 NASB).

14. Seraphim lead heaven in worship of God.

- "Seraphim stood above Him, each having six wings: with two he covered his face, and with two he covered his feet, and with two he flew. And one called out to another and said, 'Holy, Holy, Holy, is the LORD of hosts, the whole earth is full of His glory.' And the foundations of the thresholds trembled at the voice of him who called out, while the temple was filling with smoke. Then I said, 'Woe is me, for I am ruined! Because I am a man of unclean lips, and I live among a people of unclean lips; For my eyes have seen the King, the LORD of hosts.' Then one of the seraphim flew to me with a burning coal in his hand, which he had taken from the altar with tongs. He touched my mouth with it and said, 'Behold, this has touched your lips; and your iniquity is taken away and your sin is forgiven'" (Isaiah 6:2–7 NASB).

15. Michael is the archangel.

- "For the Lord Himself will descend from heaven with a shout, with the voice of the archangel and with the trumpet of God, and the dead in Christ will rise first" (1 Thessalonians 4:16 NASB).

- "But Michael the archangel, when he disputed with the devil and argued about the body of Moses, did not dare pronounce against him a railing judgment, but said, 'The Lord rebuke you!'" (Jude 9 NASB).

16. Gabriel is an announcing angel.

- "And I heard the voice of a man between the banks of Ulai, and he called out and said, 'Gabriel, give this man an understanding of the vision'" (Daniel 8:16 NASB).

- "While I was still speaking in prayer, then the man Gabriel, whom I had seen in the vision previously, came to me in my extreme weariness about the time of the evening offering. He gave me instruction and talked with me and said, 'O Daniel, I have now come forth to give you insight with understanding'" (Daniel 9:21–22 NASB).

- "The angel answered and said to him, 'I am Gabriel, who stands in the presence of God, and I have been sent to speak to you and to bring you this good news'" (Luke 1:19 NASB).

- "Now in the sixth month the angel Gabriel was sent from God to a city in Galilee called Nazareth, to a virgin engaged to a man whose name was Joseph, of the descendants of David; and the virgin's name was Mary. And coming in, he said to her, 'Greetings, favored one! The Lord is with you'" (Luke 1:26–28 NASB).

17. Angels worship God.

   - "Ascribe to the LORD, O sons of the mighty, ascribe to the LORD glory and strength. Ascribe to the LORD the glory due to His name; worship the LORD in holy array" (Psalm 29:1–2 NASB).

18. Angels rejoice in God's works.

   - "When the morning stars sang together and all the sons of God shouted for joy?" (Job 38:7 NASB).

   - "In the same way, I tell you, there is joy in the presence of the angels of God over one sinner who repents" (Luke 15:10 NASB).

19. Angels execute God's will.

   - "Bless the LORD, you His angels, mighty in strength, who perform His word, obeying the voice of His word! Bless the LORD, all you His hosts, you who serve Him, doing His will" (Psalm 103:20–21 NASB).

   - "And behold, a severe earthquake had occurred, for an angel of the Lord descended from heaven and came and rolled away the stone and sat upon it" (Matthew 28:2 NASB).

   - "In these lay a great multitude of sick people, blind, lame, paralyzed, waiting for the moving of the water. For an angel went down at a certain time into the pool and stirred up the water; then whoever stepped in first, after the stirring of the water, was made well of whatever disease he had" (John 5:3–4 NKJV).

   - "Then another angel, the one who has power over fire, came out from the altar; and he called with a loud voice to him who had the sharp sickle, saying, 'Put in your sharp sickle and gather the clusters from the vine of the earth, because her grapes are ripe.' So the angel swung his sickle to the earth and gathered the clusters from the vine of the earth, and threw them into the great wine press of the wrath of God" (Revelation 14:18–19 NASB).

20. Angels guide in the affairs of nations.

- "Then he said to me, 'Do not be afraid, Daniel, for from the first day that you set your heart on understanding this and on humbling yourself before your God, your words were heard, and I have come in response to your words. But the prince of the kingdom of Persia was withstanding me for twenty-one days; then behold, Michael, one of the chief princes, came to help me, for I had been left there with the kings of Persia. Now I have come to give you an understanding of what will happen to your people in the latter days, for the vision pertains to the days yet future'" (Daniel 10:12–14 NASB).

- "Then he said, 'Do you understand why I came to you? But I shall now return to fight against the prince of Persia; so I am going forth, and behold, the prince of Greece is about to come. However, I will tell you what is inscribed in the writing of truth yet there is no one who stands firmly with me against these forces except Michael your prince'" (Daniel 10:20–21 NASB).

21. Angels assist and protect believers.

- "But the men [angels] reached out their hands and brought Lot into the house with them, and shut the door. They struck the men who were at the doorway of the house with blindness, both small and great, so that they wearied themselves trying to find the doorway" (Genesis 19:10–11 NASB).

- "He lay down and slept under a juniper tree; and behold, there was an angel touching him, and he said to him, 'Arise, eat.' Then he looked and behold, there was at his head a bread cake baked on hot stones, and a jar of water. So he ate and drank and lay down again. The angel of the LORD came again a second time and touched him and said, 'Arise, eat, because the journey is too great for you'" (1 Kings 19:5–7 NASB).

- "The angel of the LORD encamps around those who fear Him, and rescues them" (Psalm 34:7 NASB).

- "For He will give His angels charge concerning you, to guard you in all your ways. They will bear you up in their hands, that you do not strike your foot against a stone. You will tread upon the lion and cobra, the young lion and the serpent you will trample down" (Psalm 91:11–13 NASB).

- "Then Daniel spoke to the king, 'O king, live forever! My God sent His angel and shut the lions' mouths and they have not harmed me, inasmuch as I was found innocent before Him; and also toward you, O king, I have committed no crime'" (Daniel 6:21–22 NASB).

- "Then the devil left Him; and behold, angels came and began to minister to Him" (Matthew 4:11 NASB).

22. Angels punish God's enemies.

- "Then it happened that night that the angel of the LORD went out and struck 185,000 in the camp of the Assyrians; and when men rose early in the morning, behold, all of them were dead" (2 Kings 19:35 NASB).

- "And immediately an angel of the Lord struck him because he did not give God the glory, and he was eaten by worms and died" (Acts 12:23 NASB).

23. Fallen angels, or demons, are kept in prison.

- "For if God did not spare angels when they sinned, but cast them into hell and committed them to pits of darkness, reserved for judgment . . ." (2 Peter 2:4 NASB).

- "And angels who did not keep their own domain, but abandoned their proper abode, He has kept in eternal bonds under darkness for the judgment of the great day" (Jude 6 NASB).

24. Evil angels are sometimes free.

- "He sent upon them His burning anger, fury and indignation and trouble, a band of destroying angels" (Psalm 78:49 NASB).

- "For I am convinced that neither death, nor life, nor angels, nor principalities, nor things present, nor things to come, nor powers, nor height, nor depth, nor any other created thing, will be able to separate us from the love of God, which is in Christ Jesus our Lord" (Romans 8:38–39).

- "There was war in heaven. Michael and his angels fought against the dragon, and the dragon and his angels fought back. But he was not strong enough, and they lost their place in heaven. The great dragon was hurled down—that ancient serpent called the devil, or Satan, who leads the whole world astray. He was hurled to the earth, and his angels with him" (Revelation 12:7–9).

25. Evil angels oppose God and strive to thwart his will.

- "Then he showed me Joshua the high priest standing before the angel of the LORD, and Satan standing at his right hand to accuse him. The LORD said to Satan, 'The LORD rebuke you, Satan! Indeed, the LORD who has chosen Jerusalem rebuke you! Is this not a brand plucked from the fire?'" (Zechariah 3:1–2 NASB).

- "And the enemy who sowed them is the devil, and the harvest is the end of the age; and the reapers are angels" (Matthew 13:39 NASB).

- "Be of sober spirit, be on the alert. Your adversary, the devil, prowls around like a roaring lion, seeking someone to devour" (1 Peter 5:8 NASB).

26. Evil angels hinder people's temporal welfare.

- "Then the LORD said to Satan, 'Behold, all that he has is in your power, only do not put forth your hand on him.' So Satan departed from the presence of the LORD. Now on the day when his sons and his daughters were eating and drinking wine in their oldest brother's house, a messenger came to Job and said, 'The oxen were plowing and the donkeys feeding beside them, and the Sabeans attacked and took them. They also slew the servants with the edge of the sword, and I alone have escaped to tell you.' While he was still speaking, another also came and said, 'The fire of God fell from heaven and burned up the sheep and the servants and consumed them, and I alone have escaped to tell you.' While he was still speaking, another also came and said, 'The Chaldeans formed three bands and made a raid on the camels and took them and slew the servants with the edge of the sword, and I alone have escaped to tell you.' While he was still speaking, another also came and said, 'Your sons and your daughters were eating and drinking wine in their oldest brother's house, and behold, a great wind came from across the wilderness and struck the four corners of the house, and it fell on the young people and they died, and I alone have escaped to tell you'" (Job 1:12–19 NASB).

- "Then Satan went out from the presence of the LORD and smote Job with sore boils from the sole of his foot to the crown of his head. And he took a potsherd to scrape himself while he was sitting among the ashes" (Job 2:7–8 NASB).

- "One Sabbath day as Jesus was teaching in a synagogue, he saw a woman who had been crippled by an evil spirit. She had been bent double for eighteen years and was unable to stand up straight. . . . 'Wasn't it necessary for me, even on the Sabbath day, to free this dear woman from the bondage in which Satan has held her for eighteen years?'" (Luke 13:10–11, 16 NLT).

- ". . . even though I have received wonderful revelations from God. But to keep me from getting puffed up, I was given a thorn in my flesh, a messenger from Satan to torment me and keep me from getting proud" (2 Corinthians 12:7 NLT).

- "We wanted very much to come, and I, Paul, tried again and again, but Satan prevented us" (1 Thessalonians 2:18 NLT).

27. Power of evil spirits over humans is not independent of people's will.

   - "Put on all of God's armor so that you will be able to stand firm against all strategies and tricks of the Devil" (Ephesians 6:11 NLT).

   - "In every battle you will need faith as your shield to stop the fiery arrows aimed at you by Satan" (Ephesians 6:16 NLT).

   - "So humble yourselves before God. Resist the Devil, and he will flee from you" (James 4:7 NLT).

28. Evil angels are destined for punishment.

   - "Then the King will turn to those on the left and say, 'Away with you, you cursed ones, into the eternal fire prepared for the Devil and his demons!'" (Matthew 25:41 NLT).

   - "Then the Devil, who betrayed them, was thrown into the lake of fire that burns with sulfur, joining the beast and the false prophet. There they will be tormented day and night forever and ever" (Revelation 20:10 NLT).

■ LIST #29
7 Things to Know about Satan

Satan began as a glorious angel, but he rebelled against God and was cast out of heaven.

1. Names and Descriptors of Satan

- Abaddon / Apollyon—Revelation 9:11
- Accuser—Revelation 12:10
- Adversary—1 Peter 5:8 KJV
- Ancient serpent—Revelation 12:9
- Angel of the Abyss—Revelation 9:11
- Beelzebub—Matthew 12:24
- Belial—2 Corinthians 6:15
- Devil—Matthew 4:1
- Enemy—Matthew 13:39
- The evil one—Matthew 13:19, 38
- Evil spirit—1 Samuel 16:14; Matthew 12:43
- Father of lies—John 8:44
- God of this age—2 Corinthians 4:4
- Great red dragon—Revelation 12:3, 9
- Liar—John 8:44
- Lucifer—Isaiah 14:12 KJV

- Morning star—Isaiah 14:12

- Prince of demons—Matthew 12:24

- Prince of this world—John 12:31

- Ruler of the kingdom of the air—Ephesians 2:2

- Satan—1 Chronicles 21:1

- Serpent—Genesis 3:4

- Son of the dawn—Isaiah 14:12

- Spirit who is now at work in those who are disobedient—Ephesians 2:2

- The tempter—Matthew 4:3

2. Satan's Origin

"Son of man, weep for the king of Tyre. Give him this message from the Sovereign LORD: You were the perfection of wisdom and beauty. You were in Eden, the garden of God. Your clothing was adorned with every precious stone—red carnelian, chrysolite, white moonstone, beryl, onyx, jasper, sapphire, turquoise, and emerald—all beautifully crafted for you and set in the finest gold. They were given to you on the day you were created. I ordained and anointed you as the mighty angelic guardian. You had access to the holy mountain of God and walked among the stones of fire" (Ezekiel 28:12–14 NLT).

3. Satan's Fall

"You were blameless in all you did from the day you were created until the day evil was found in you. Your great wealth filled you with violence, and you sinned. So

I banished you from the mountain of God. I expelled you, O mighty guardian, from your place among the stones of fire. Your heart was filled with pride because of all your beauty. You corrupted your wisdom for the sake of your splendor. So I threw you to the earth and exposed you to the curious gaze of kings" (Ezekiel 28:15–17 NLT).

4. Satan's Personality

"For you said to yourself, 'I will ascend to heaven and set my throne above God's stars. I will preside on the mountain of the gods far away in the north. I will climb to the highest heavens and be like the Most High'" (Isaiah 14:13–14 NLT).

"Your heart was filled with pride because of all your beauty. You corrupted your wisdom for the sake of your splendor. So I threw you to the earth and exposed you to the curious gaze of kings" (Ezekiel 28:17 NLT).

"Rejoice, O heavens! And you who live in the heavens, rejoice! But terror will come on the earth and the sea. For the Devil has come down to you in great anger, and he knows that he has little time" (Revelation 12:12 NLT).

5. Satan's Dwelling Place

In heavenly realms

"For we are not fighting against people made of flesh and blood, but against the evil rulers and authorities of the unseen world, against those mighty powers of darkness who rule this world, and against wicked spirits in the heavenly realms" (Ephesians 6:12 NLT).

"One day the angels came to present themselves before the LORD, and Satan the Accuser came with them" (Job 1:6 NLT).

In the air

"You used to live just like the rest of the world, full of sin, obeying Satan, the mighty prince of the power of the air. He is the spirit at work in the hearts of those who refuse to obey God" (Ephesians 2:2 NLT).

On the earth

"Where have you come from?" the LORD asked Satan. And Satan answered the LORD, "I have been going back and forth across the earth, watching everything that's going on" (Job 1:7 NLT).

His future dwelling place

"Then the King will turn to those on the left and say, 'Away with you, you cursed ones, into the eternal fire prepared for the Devil and his demons!'" (Matthew 25:41 NLT).

"But instead, you will be brought down to the place of the dead, down to its lowest depths" (Isaiah 14:15 NLT).

6. Satan's Work

Keeps unbelievers from Christ.

"Satan, the god of this evil world, has blinded the minds of those who don't believe, so they are unable to see the glorious light of the Good News that is shining upon them. They don't understand the message we preach about the glory of Christ, who is the exact likeness of God" (2 Corinthians 4:4 NLT).

Tempts and hinders Christians.

"Then Peter said, 'Ananias, why has Satan filled your heart? You lied to the Holy Spirit, and you kept some of the money for yourself'" (Acts 5:3 NLT).

"Be careful! Watch out for attacks from the Devil, your

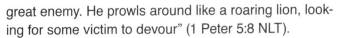

great enemy. He prowls around like a roaring lion, looking for some victim to devour" (1 Peter 5:8 NLT).

Accuses believers before God.

"Then I heard a loud voice shouting across the heavens, 'It has happened at last—the salvation and power and kingdom of our God, and the authority of his Christ! For the Accuser has been thrown down to earth—the one who accused our brothers and sisters before our God day and night'" (Revelation 12:10 NLT).

7. Admonitions about Satan

Be watchful.

"Be careful! Watch out for attacks from the Devil, your great enemy. He prowls around like a roaring lion, looking for some victim to devour. Take a firm stand against him, and be strong in your faith. Remember that your Christian brothers and sisters all over the world are going through the same kind of suffering you are" (1 Peter 5:8–9 NLT).

Put on the armor of God.

"Put on all of God's armor so that you will be able to stand firm against all strategies of the devil. For we are not fighting against flesh-and-blood enemies, but against evil rulers and authorities of the unseen world, against mighty powers in this dark world, and against evil spirits in the heavenly places. Therefore, put on every piece of God's armor so you will be able to resist the enemy in the time of evil. Then after the battle you will still be standing firm. Stand your ground, putting on the belt of truth and the body armor of God's righteousness. For shoes, put on the peace that comes from the Good News so that you will be fully prepared. In addition to all of these, hold up the shield of faith to stop the fiery arrows of the devil" (Ephesians 6:11–18 NLT).

Resist Satan.

"So humble yourselves before God. Resist the Devil, and he will flee from you. Draw close to God, and God will draw close to you. Wash your hands, you sinners; purify your hearts, you hypocrites. Let there be tears for the wrong things you have done. Let there be sorrow and deep grief. Let there be sadness instead of laughter, and gloom instead of joy. When you bow down before the Lord and admit your dependence on him, he will lift you up and give you honor" (James 4:7–10 NLT).

■ LIST #30
9 Principles of Peace

Peace is much talked about in the world. But what is peace?

National peace is freedom from war or civil strife. Legal peace is security, law and order, and freedom from public disturbance. Psychological peace is harmony, friendship, and freedom from disagreement or quarrels. Practical peace is an undisturbed state of mind, an absence of mental conflict, and serenity.

Theological peace is to be joined together as one with God—to be in quietness and rest as a friend of God. Do you have this peace? The God of peace would like to give it to you.

Consider a few things the Bible has to say about peace.

1. "For the Scriptures say, 'If you want a happy life and good days, keep your tongue from speaking evil, and keep your lips from telling lies. Turn away from evil and do good. Work hard at living in peace with others'" (1 Peter 3:10–11 NLT).

2. "So then, let us aim for harmony in the church and try to build each other up" (Romans 14:19 NLT).

3. "Live in harmony with each other. Don't try to act important, but enjoy the company of ordinary people. And don't think you know it all! Do your part to live in peace with everyone, as much as possible. Don't let evil get the best of you, but conquer evil by doing good" (Romans 12:16, 18, 21 NLT).

4. "Try to live in peace with everyone, and seek to live a clean and holy life, for those who are not holy will not see the Lord. Look after each other so that none of you will miss out on the special favor of God. Watch out that no bitter root of unbelief rises up among you, for whenever it springs up, many are corrupted by its poison" (Hebrews 12:14–15 NLT).

5. "But the wisdom that comes from heaven is first of all pure. It is also peace loving, gentle at all times, and willing to yield to others. It is full of mercy and good deeds. It shows no partiality and is always sincere. And those who are peacemakers will plant seeds of peace and reap a harvest of goodness" (James 3:17–18 NLT).

6. "Therefore, since we have been made right in God's sight by faith, we have peace with God because of what Jesus Christ our Lord has done for us. Because of our faith, Christ has brought us into this place of highest privilege where we now stand, and we confidently and joyfully look forward to sharing God's glory" (Romans 5:1–2 NLT).

7. "So I pray that God, who gives you hope, will keep you happy and full of peace as you believe in him. May you overflow with hope through the power of the Holy Spirit" (Romans 15:13 NLT).

8. "Always be full of joy in the Lord. I say it again—rejoice! Let everyone see that you are considerate in all you do. Remember, the Lord is coming soon. Don't worry about anything; instead, pray about everything. Tell God what you need, and thank him for all he has done. If you do this, you will experience God's peace, which is far more wonderful than the human mind

can understand. His peace will guard your hearts and minds as you live in Christ Jesus. And now, dear brothers and sisters, let me say one more thing as I close this letter. Fix your thoughts on what is true and honorable and right. Think about things that are pure and lovely and admirable. Think about things that are excellent and worthy of praise. Keep putting into practice all you learned from me and heard from me and saw me doing, and the God of peace will be with you" (Philippians 4:4–9 NLT).

9. "And let the peace that comes from Christ rule in your hearts. For as members of one body you are all called to live in peace. And always be thankful" (Colossians 3:15 NLT).

■ LIST #31
4 Things to Remember about Jealousy

Few things can wreak havoc with one's emotions more than jealousy. It's a canker and a cancer that can destroy our happiness and joy. Consider what the Bible says about jealousy.

1. "A relaxed attitude lengthens life; jealousy rots it away" (Proverbs 14:30 NLT).

2. "Do not fret because of evildoers; don't envy the wicked. For the evil have no future; their light will be snuffed out" (Proverbs 24:19–20 NLT).

3. "Love is patient and kind. Love is not jealous or boastful or proud" (1 Corinthians 13:4 NLT).

4. "If you are wise and understand God's ways, live a life of steady goodness so that only good deeds will pour forth. And if you don't brag about the good you do, then you will be truly wise! But if you are bitterly jealous and there is selfish ambition in your hearts, don't brag about being wise. That is the worst kind of lie. For jealousy and selfishness are not God's kind of wisdom. Such things are earthly, unspiritual, and motivated by the Devil. For wherever there is jealousy and selfish ambition, there you will find disorder and every kind of evil" (James 3:14–16 NLT).

■ LIST #32
6 Affirmations of a Clear Conscience

If you want to have ultimate freedom, you can start by having a clear conscience. A clear conscience gives you confidence, boldness, and peace, as we see in the scriptures below.

1. "Gazing intently at the high council, Paul began: 'Brothers, I have always lived before God in all good conscience!'" (Acts 23:1 NLT).

2. "In the same way, deacons must be people who are respected and have integrity. They must not be heavy drinkers and must not be greedy for money. They must be committed to the revealed truths of the Christian faith and must live with a clear conscience" (1 Timothy 3:8–9 NLT).

3. "Keep your conscience clear. Then if people speak evil against you, they will be ashamed when they see what a good life you live because you belong to Christ" (1 Peter 3:16 NLT).

4. "Because of this, I always try to maintain a clear conscience before God and everyone else" (Acts 24:16 NLT).

5. "Even when Gentiles, who do not have God's written law, instinctively follow what the law says, they show that in their hearts they know right from wrong. They demonstrate that God's law is written within them, for their own consciences either accuse them or tell them they are doing what is right" (Romans 2:14–15 NLT).

6. "And since we have a great High Priest who rules over God's people, let us go right into the presence of God, with true hearts fully trusting him. For our evil consciences have been sprinkled with Christ's blood to make us clean, and our bodies have been washed with pure water" (Hebrews 10:21–22 NLT).

LIST #33
6 Women of the Night

It has been said that prostitution is the oldest profession in the world. The first book in the Bible mentions it, and even the last book in the Bible talks about a figurative "great prostitute."

1. "Someone told Tamar that her father-in-law had left for the sheep-shearing at Timnah. Tamar was aware that Shelah had grown up, but they had not called her to come and marry him. So she changed out of her widow's clothing and covered herself with a veil to disguise herself. Then she sat beside the road at the entrance to the village of Enaim, which is on the way to Timnah. Judah noticed her as he went by and thought she was a prostitute, since her face was veiled. So he stopped and propositioned her to sleep with him, not realizing that she was his own daughter-in-law" (Genesis 38:13–16 NLT).

2. "Then Joshua secretly sent out two spies from the Israelite camp at Acacia. He instructed them, 'Spy out the land on the other side of the Jordan River, especially around Jericho.' So the two men set out and came to the house of a prostitute named Rahab and stayed there that night" (Joshua 2:1 NLT).

3. "Now Jephthah of Gilead was a great warrior. He was the son of Gilead, but his mother was a prostitute" (Judges 11:1 NLT).

4. "One day Samson went to the Philistine city of Gaza and spent the night with a prostitute" (Judges 16:1 NLT).

5. "Some time later, two prostitutes came to the king to have an argument settled. 'Please, my lord,' one of them began, 'this woman and I live in the same house. I gave birth to a baby while she was with me in the house. Three days later, she also had a baby. We were alone; there were only two of us in the house. But her baby died during the night when she rolled over on it. Then she got up in the night and took my son from beside me while I was asleep. She laid her dead child in my arms and took mine to sleep beside her. And in the morning when I tried to nurse my son, he was dead! But when I looked more closely in the morning light, I saw that it wasn't my son at all.' Then the other woman interrupted, 'It certainly was your son, and the living child is mine.' 'No,' the first woman said, 'The dead one is yours, and the living one is mine.' And so they argued back and forth before the king. Then the king said, 'Let's get the facts straight. Both of you claim the living child is yours, and each says that the dead child belongs to the other. All right, bring me a sword.' So a sword was brought to the king. Then he said, 'Cut the living child in two and give half to each of these women!' Then the woman who really was the mother of the living child, and who loved him very much, cried out, 'Oh no, my lord! Give her the child—please do not kill him!' But the other woman said, 'All right, he will be neither yours nor mine; divide him between us!' Then the king said, 'Do not kill him, but give the baby to the woman who wants him to live, for she is his mother!'" (1 Kings 3:16–27 NLT).

6. "One of the seven angels who had poured out the
   seven bowls came over and spoke to me. 'Come
   with me,' he said, 'and I will show you the judgment
   that is going to come on the great prostitute, who sits
   on many waters. The rulers of the world have had
   immoral relations with her, and the people who belong
   to this world have been made drunk by the wine of her
   immorality'" (Revelation 17:1–2 NLT).

LIST #34
11 Scriptures about Family Living

God is concerned about family life. He gives us clear thinking about sex, whom we should marry, and the roles of husbands, wives, and children.

1. The spouses' sexual relationship

   "But because there is so much sexual immorality, each man should have his own wife, and each woman should have her own husband. The husband should not deprive his wife of sexual intimacy, which is her right as a married woman, nor should the wife deprive her husband. The wife gives authority over her body to her husband, and the husband also gives authority over his body to his wife. So do not deprive each other of sexual relations. The only exception to this rule would be the agreement of both husband and wife to refrain from sexual intimacy for a limited time, so they can give themselves more completely to prayer. Afterward they should come together again so that Satan won't be able to tempt them because of their lack of self-control" (1 Corinthians 7:2–5 NLT).

2. Divorce

   "Now, for those who are married I have a command that comes not from me, but from the Lord. A wife must not leave her husband. But if she does leave him, let her remain single or else go back to him. And the husband must not leave his wife. Now, I will speak to the rest of you, though I do not have a direct command from the Lord. If a Christian man has a wife who is an unbeliever and she is willing to continue living with him, he must not leave her. And if a Christian woman has a husband who is an unbeliever, and he is willing to continue living with her, she must not leave him. For the Christian wife brings holiness to her marriage, and the Christian husband brings holiness to his marriage. Otherwise, your children would not have a godly influence, but now they are set apart for him. (But if the husband or wife who isn't a Christian insists on leaving, let them go. In such cases the Christian husband or wife is not required to stay with them, for God wants his children to live in peace)" (1 Corinthians 7:10–15 NLT).

3. Responsibility

"But there is one thing I want you to know: A man is responsible to Christ, a woman is responsible to her husband, and Christ is responsible to God" (1 Corinthians 11:3 NLT).

4. Whom we should marry

"Don't team up with those who are unbelievers. How can goodness be a partner with wickedness? How can light live with darkness?" (2 Corinthians 6:14 NLT).

5. Children

"Children born to a young man are like sharp arrows in a warrior's hands. How happy is the man whose quiver is full of them! He will not be put to shame when he confronts his accusers at the city gates" (Psalm 127:4–5 NLT).

6. Children's obedience and parental responsibilities

"Children, obey your parents because you belong to the Lord, for this is the right thing to do. 'Honor

your father and mother.' This is the first of the Ten
Commandments that ends with a promise. And this
is the promise: If you honor your father and mother,
'you will live a long life, full of blessing.' And now a
word to you fathers. Don't make your children angry
by the way you treat them. Rather, bring them up with
the discipline and instruction approved by the Lord"
(Ephesians 6:1–4 NLT).

7. The roles of family members

"You wives must submit to your husbands, as is fitting
for those who belong to the Lord. And you husbands
must love your wives and never treat them harshly.
You children must always obey your parents, for this
is what pleases the Lord. Fathers, don't aggravate
your children. If you do, they will become discouraged
and quit trying" (Colossians 3:18–21 NLT).

8. Providing for the family

"But those who won't care for their own relatives,
especially those living in the same household, have
denied what we believe. Such people are worse than
unbelievers" (1 Timothy 5:8 NLT).

9. Widows

"So I advise these younger widows to marry again,
have children, and take care of their own homes.
Then the enemy will not be able to say anything
against them" (1 Timothy 5:14 NLT).

10. Harmony between husbands and wives

"In the same way, you wives must accept the
authority of your husbands, even those who refuse
to accept the Good News. Your godly lives will
speak to them better than any words. They will be

won over by watching your pure, godly behavior. Don't be concerned about the outward beauty that depends on fancy hairstyles, expensive jewelry, or beautiful clothes. You should be known for the beauty that comes from within, the unfading beauty of a gentle and quiet spirit, which is so precious to God. That is the way the holy women of old made themselves beautiful. They trusted God and accepted the authority of their husbands. For instance, Sarah obeyed her husband, Abraham, when she called him her master. You are her daughters when you do what is right without fear of what your husbands might do. In the same way, you husbands must give honor to your wives. Treat her with understanding as you live together. She may be weaker than you are, but she is your equal partner in God's gift of new life. If you don't treat her as you should, your prayers will not be heard" (1 Peter 3:1–7 NLT).

11. Husbands

"And you husbands must love your wives with the same love Christ showed the church. He gave up his life for her to make her holy and clean, washed by baptism and God's word" (Ephesians 5:25 NLT).

LIST #35
9 Admonitions for the Obedient Heart

Learning to submit to legitimate authority is not an easy task. It means we may have to give up our own selfish interests and desires. But the end result of obedience is self-discipline, fulfillment, and peace.

1. "This command I am giving you today is not too difficult for you to understand or perform. It is not up in heaven, so distant that you must ask, 'Who will go to heaven and bring it down so we can hear and obey it?' It is not beyond the sea, so far away that you must ask, 'Who will cross the sea to bring it to us so we can hear and obey it?' The message is very close at hand; it is on your lips and in your heart so that you can obey it. 'Now listen! Today I am giving you a choice between prosperity and disaster, between life and death. I have commanded you today to love the LORD your God and to keep his commands, laws, and regulations by walking in his ways. If you do this, you will live and become a great nation, and the LORD your God will bless you and the land you are about to enter and occupy'" (Deuteronomy 30:11–16 NLT).

2. "Reverence for the LORD is the foundation of true wisdom. The rewards of wisdom come to all who obey him. Praise his name forever!" (Psalm 111:10 NLT).

3. "Happy are those who obey his decrees and search for him with all their hearts" (Psalm 119:2 NLT).

4. "Here is my final conclusion: Fear God and obey his commands, for this is the duty of every person. God will

judge us for everything we do, including every secret thing, whether good or bad" (Ecclesiastes 12:13–14 NLT).

5. "No one can serve two masters. For you will hate one and love the other, or be devoted to one and despise the other. You cannot serve both God and money" (Matthew 6:24 NLT).

6. "If you love me, obey my commandments" (John 14:15 NLT).

7. "Those who obey my commandments are the ones who love me. And because they love me, my Father will love them, and I will love them. And I will reveal myself to each one of them" (John 14:21 NLT).

8. "Don't you realize that whatever you choose to obey becomes your master? You can choose sin, which leads to death, or you can choose to obey God and receive his approval. Thank God! Once you were slaves of sin, but now you have obeyed with all your heart the new teaching God has given you. Now you are free from sin, your old master, and you have become slaves to your new master, righteousness" (Romans 6:16–18 NLT).

9. "Dear friends, if our conscience is clear, we can come to God with bold confidence. And we will receive whatever we request because we obey him and do the things that please him. And this is his commandment: We must believe in the name of his Son, Jesus Christ, and love one another, just as he commanded us. Those who obey God's commandments live in fellowship with him, and he with them. And we know he lives in us because the Holy Spirit lives in us" (1 John 3:21–24 NLT).

■ LIST #36
16 Instruments and 13 Examples of Making Music

Music played a big part in the lives of Bible people. Here are sixteen musical instruments mentioned in the Bible, as well as some ways music was used.

Musical Instruments

1. Cymbals—2 Samuel 6:5; Nehemiah 12:27; Psalm 150:5; 1 Corinthians 13:1

2. Flute—Genesis 4:21; Job 21:12; Psalm 150:4; Jeremiah 48:36; Daniel 3:5

3. Gong—1 Corinthians 13:1

4. Harp—Genesis 4:21; 2 Samuel 6:5; Nehemiah 12:27; Job 21:12; Psalms 33:2; 150:3; Daniel 3:5

5. Horn—Daniel 3:5

6. Lute—1 Samuel 18:6; 2 Chronicles 20:28

7. Lyre—2 Samuel 6:5; Nehemiah 12:27; Psalm 150:3; Daniel 3:5

8. Pipes—Daniel 3:5

9. Ram's horn—Joshua 6:4; 1 Chronicles 15:28

10. Resounding cymbals—Psalm 150:5

11. Sistrum (U-shaped instrument that made a rattling sound)—2 Samuel 6:5

12. Strings—Psalm 150:4

13. Tambourine—2 Samuel 6:5; Job 21:12; Psalm 68:25; 150:4

14. Ten-stringed lyre—Psalm 33:2

15. Trumpet—Joshua 6:4–5; Psalm 150:3; Jeremiah 51:27

16. Zither—Daniel 3:5

Uses of Music

1. To celebrate saying good-bye—Genesis 31:27

2. To celebrate triumph over enemies—Exodus 15:20

3. To celebrate triumph in battle—Judges 11:34; 1 Samuel 18:6

4. To exorcise evil spirits—1 Samuel 16:23; 18:10

5. To soothe—1 Samuel 16:23

6. To go before the ark of God—1 Chronicles 15:15–16, 27

7. To thank and praise God—1 Chronicles 25:3

8. For going into battle—2 Chronicles 20:21

9. To commemorate and honor the dead—2 Chronicles 35:25

10. For dedications—Ezra 3:10

11. To mock—Job 30:9

12. To praise God—Psalm 98:4–6

13. To announce the Second Coming—1 Thessalonians 4:16–18

LIST #37
30 Financial Principles

The Bible has a great deal to say about our attitude toward money. When applied, the Bible's principles toward money will transform our thinking and will bring security to our lives.

1. Principle of acknowledgment
   - "True humility and fear of the LORD lead to riches, honor, and long life" (Proverbs 22:4 NLT).

2. Principle of attitude
   - "Some who are poor pretend to be rich; others who are rich pretend to be poor" (Proverbs 13:7 NLT).

3. Principle of blessing
   - "How joyful are those who fear the Lord—all who follow his ways! You will enjoy the fruit of your labor. How joyful and prosperous you will be!" (Psalm 128:1–2 NLT).

4. Principle of contentment
   - "Better to have little, with fear for the Lord, than to have great treasure and inner turmoil" (Proverbs 15:16 NLT).
   - "It is better to be godly and have little than to be evil and rich" (Psalm 37:16 NLT).
   - "O God, I beg two favors from you; let me have them before I die. First, help me never to tell a lie. Second, give me neither poverty nor riches! Give me just enough to satisfy my needs.

For if I grow rich, I may deny you and say, 'Who is the Lord?' And if I am too poor, I may steal and thus insult God's holy name" (Proverbs 30:7–9 NLT).

- "Even so, I have noticed one thing, at least, that is good. It is good for people to eat, drink, and enjoy their work under the sun during the short life God has given them, and to accept their lot in life. And it is a good thing to receive wealth from God and the good health to enjoy it. To enjoy your work and accept your lot in life—this is indeed a gift from God. God keeps such people so busy enjoying life that they take no time to brood over the past" (Ecclesiastes 5:18–20 NLT).

5. Principle of credit

- "Just as the rich rule the poor, so the borrower is servant to the lender" (Proverbs 22:7 NLT).

6. Principle of consulting

- "Fools think their own way is right, but the wise listen to others" (Proverbs 12:15 NLT).

- "Plans succeed through good counsel; don't go to war without wise advice" (Proverbs 20:18 NLT).

7. Principle of charity

- "If someone has enough money to live well and sees a brother or sister in need but shows no compassion—how can God's love be in that person? Dear children, let's not merely say that we love each other; let us show the truth by our actions" (1 John 3:17–18 NLT).

8. Principle of end results

- "Don't store up treasures here on earth, where

moths eat them and rust destroys them, and where thieves break in and steal. Store your treasures in heaven, where moths and rust cannot destroy, and thieves do not break in and steal. Wherever your treasure is, there the desires of your heart will also be" (Matthew 6:19–21 NLT).

- "Young people, it's wonderful to be young! Enjoy every minute of it. Do everything you want to do; take it all in. But remember that you must give an account to God for everything you do. So refuse to worry, and keep your body healthy. But remember that youth, with a whole life before you, is meaningless" (Ecclesiastes 11:9–10 NLT).

- "That's the whole story. Here now is my final conclusion: Fear God and obey his commands, for this is everyone's duty" (Ecclesiastes 12:13–14 NLT).

9. Principle of dependence

- "Trust in your money and down you go! But the godly flourish like leaves in spring" (Proverbs 11:28 NLT).

10. Principle of diligence

- "Riches can disappear fast. And the king's crown doesn't stay in his family forever—so watch your business interests closely. Know the state of your flocks and your herds; then there will be lamb's wool enough for clothing, and goat's milk enough for food for all your household after the hay is harvested, and the new crop appears, and the mountain grasses are gathered in" (Proverbs 27:23–27 TLB).

11. Principle of endorsement

- "The world's poorest credit risk is the man who

agrees to pay a stranger's debts" (Proverbs 27:13 TLB).

- "If you endorse a note for someone you hardly know, guaranteeing his debt, you are in serious trouble. You may have trapped yourself by your agreement. Quick! Get out of it if you possibly can! Swallow your pride; don't let embarrassment stand in the way. Go and beg to have your name erased. Don't put it off. Do it now. Don't rest until you do. If you can get out of this trap you have saved yourself like a deer that escapes from a hunter, or a bird from the net" (Proverbs 6:1–5 TLB).

12. Principle of first cause

- "Whatever is good and perfect comes down to us from God our Father, who created all the lights in the heavens. He never changes or casts a shifting shadow" (James 1:17 NLT).

- "Remember the Lord your God. He is the one who gives you power to be successful, in order to fulfill the covenant he confirmed to your ancestors with an oath" (Deuteronomy 8:18 NLT).

- "This is what the LORD says: 'Don't let the wise boast in their wisdom, or the powerful boast in their power, or the rich boast in their riches. But those who wish to boast should boast in this alone: that they truly know me and understand that I am the LORD who demonstrates unfailing love and who brings justice and righteousness to the earth, and that I delight in these things. I, the LORD, have spoken!'" (Jeremiah 9:23–24 NLT).

- "For what gives you the right to make such a judgment? What do you have that God hasn't given you? And if everything you have is from God, why boast as though it were not a gift?" (1 Corinthians 4:7 NLT).

13. Principle of focus

- "No one can serve two masters. For you will hate one and love the other; you will be devoted to one and despise the other. You cannot serve both God and money" (Matthew 6:24 NLT).

- "This should be your ambition: to live a quiet life, minding your own business and doing your own work, just as we told you before. As a result, people who are not Christians will trust and respect you, and you will not need to depend on others for enough money to pay your bills" (1 Thessalonians 4:11–12 TLB).

14. Principle of gambling

- "Wealth from gambling quickly disappears; wealth from hard work grows" (Proverbs 13:11 TLB).

15. Principle of getting rich quick

- "Trying to get rich quick is evil and leads to poverty" (Proverbs 28:22 TLB).

16. Principle of giving

- "'Should people cheat God? Yet you have cheated me! But you ask, "What do you mean? When did we ever cheat you?" You have cheated me of the tithes and offerings due to me. Bring all the tithes into the storehouse so there will be enough food in my Temple. If you do,' says the Lord of Heaven's Armies, 'I will open the windows of heaven for you. I will pour out a blessing so great you won't have enough room to take it in!'" (Malachi 3:8, 10 NLT).

- "Honor the Lord with your wealth and with the best part of everything you produce. Then he will fill your barns with grain, and your vats will overflow with good wine" (Proverbs 3:9–10 NLT).

- "Give, and you will receive. Your gift will return to you in full—pressed down, shaken together to make room for more, running over, and poured into your lap. The amount you give will determine the amount you get back" (Luke 6:38 NLT).

- "But when you give to someone in need, don't let your left hand know what your right hand is doing. Give your gifts in private, and your Father, who sees everything, will reward you" (Matthew 6:3–4 NLT).

17. Principle of greed

- "Yet true godliness with contentment is itself great wealth. After all, we brought nothing with us when we came into the world, and we can't take anything with us when we leave it. So if we have enough food and clothing, let us be content. But people who long to be rich fall into temptation and are trapped by many foolish and harmful desires that plunge them into ruin and destruction. For the love of money is the root of all kinds of evil. And some people, craving money, have wandered from the true faith and pierced themselves with many sorrows" (1 Timothy 6:6–10 NLT).

- "Then he said, 'Beware! Guard against every kind of greed. Life is not measured by how much you own'" (Luke 12:15 NLT).

- "Those who love money will never have enough. How meaningless to think that wealth brings true happiness!" (Ecclesiastes 5:10 NLT).

18. Principle of hard work

- "Lazy people are soon poor; hard workers get rich" (Proverbs 10:4 NLT).

- "Work brings profit, but mere talk leads to poverty!" (Proverbs 14:23 NLT).

- "A hard worker has plenty of food but a person who chases fantasies ends up in poverty" (Proverbs 28:19 NLT).

- "An empty stable stays clean—but there is no income from an empty stable" (Proverbs 14:4 TLB).

- "Even while we were with you, we gave you this command: 'Those unwilling to work will not get to eat'" (2 Thessalonians 3:10 NLT).

19. Principle of honesty

- "Better to have little, with godliness, than to be rich and dishonest" (Proverbs 16:8 NLT).

- "Wealth created by a lying tongue is a vanishing mist and a deadly trap" (Proverbs 21:6 NLT).

- "If you are faithful in little things, you will be faithful in large ones. But if you are dishonest in little things, you won't be honest with greater responsibilities. And if you are untrustworthy about worldly wealth, who will trust you with the true riches of heaven? And if you are not faithful with other people's things, why should you be trusted with things of your own?" (Luke 16:10–12 NLT).

20. Principle of kindness

- "Give freely and become more wealthy; be stingy and lose everything. The generous will

prosper; those who refresh others will themselves be refreshed" (Proverbs 11:24–25 NLT).

- "When you harvest the crops of your land, do not harvest the grain along the edges of your fields, and do not pick up what the harvesters drop. It is the same with your grape crop—do not strip every last bunch of grapes from the vines, and do not pick up the grapes that fall to the ground. Leave them for the poor and the foreigners living among you. I am the Lord your God" (Leviticus 19:9–10 NLT).

- "Teach those who are rich in this world not to be proud and not to trust in their money, which is so unreliable. Their trust should be in God, who richly gives us all we need for our enjoyment. Tell them to use their money to do good. They should be rich in good works and generous to those in need, always being ready to share with others. By doing this they will be storing up their treasure as a good foundation for the future so that they may experience true life" (1 Timothy 6:17–19 NLT).

- "And I have been a constant example of how you can help those in need by working hard. You should remember the words of the Lord Jesus: 'It is more blessed to give than to receive'" (Acts 20:35 NLT).

21. Principle of paying taxes

- "'Now tell us what you think about this: Is it right to pay taxes to Caesar or not?' 'Here, show me the coin used for the tax.' When they handed him a Roman coin, he asked, 'Whose picture and title are stamped on it?' 'Caesar's,' they replied. 'Well, then,' he said, 'give to Caesar what belongs to Caesar, and give to God what belongs to God'" (Matthew 22:17, 19–21 NLT).

- "Pay your taxes, too, for these same reasons. For government workers need to be paid. They are serving God in what they do. Give to everyone what you owe them: Pay your taxes and government fees to those who collect them, and give respect and honor to those who are in authority" (Romans 13:6–7 NLT).

22. Principle of perspective

- "Do not be dismayed when evil men grow rich and build their lovely homes. For when they die they carry nothing with them! Their honors will not follow them. Though a man calls himself happy all through his life—and the world loudly applauds success— yet in the end he dies like everyone else, and enters eternal darkness. For man with all his pomp must die like any animal" (Psalm 49:16–20 TLB).

- "The rich man thinks of his wealth as an impregnable defense, a high wall of safety. What a dreamer!" (Proverbs 18:11 TLB).

- "Don't wear yourself out trying to get rich. Be wise enough to know when to quit. In the blink of an eye wealth disappears, for it will sprout wings and fly away like an eagle" (Proverbs 23:4–5 NLT).

23. Principle of satisfaction

- "People who work hard sleep well, whether they eat little or much. But the rich seldom get a good night's sleep" (Ecclesiastes 5:12 NLT).

24. Principle of saving

   - "The wise man saves for the future, but the fool-ish man spends whatever he gets" (Proverbs 21:20 TLB).

25. Principle of sowing and reaping

   - "Remember this—if you give little, you will get little. A farmer who plants just a few seeds will get only a small crop, but if he plants much, he will reap much. Every one must make up his own mind as to how much he should give. Don't force anyone to give more than he really wants to, for cheerful givers are the ones God prizes. God is able to make it up to you by giving you everything you need and more, so that there will not only be enough for your own needs, but plenty left over to give joyfully to others. It is as the Scriptures say: 'The godly man gives generously to the poor. His good deeds will be an honor to him for-ever.' For God, who gives seed to the farmer to plant, and later on, good crops to harvest and eat, will give you more and more seed to plant and will make it grow so that you can give away more and more fruit from your harvest. Yes, God will give you much so that you can give away much, and when we take your gifts to those who need them they will break out into thanksgiving and praise to God for your help. So, two good things happen as a result of your gifts—those in need are helped, and they overflow with thanks to God. Those you help will be glad not only because of your generous gifts to themselves and to others, but they will praise God for this proof that your deeds are as good as your doctrine" (2 Corinthians 9:6–13 TLB).

26. Principle of speculation

- "Good planning and hard work lead to prosperity, but hasty shortcuts lead to poverty" (Proverbs 21:5 NLT).

- "There is another serious problem I have seen under the sun. Hoarding riches harms the saver. Money is put into risky investments that turn sour, and everything is lost. In the end, there is nothing left to pass on to one's children. We all come to the end of our lives as naked and empty-handed as on the day we were born. We can't take our riches with us. And this, too, is a very serious problem. People leave this world no better off than when they came. All their hard work is for nothing—like working for the wind. Throughout their lives, they live under a cloud—frustrated, discouraged, and angry" (Ecclesiastes 5:13–17 NLT).

27. Principle of spending

- "The more you have, the more you spend, right up to the limits of your income, so what is the advantage of wealth—except perhaps to watch it as it runs through your fingers!" (Ecclesiastes 5:11 TLB).

28. Principle of thanksgiving

- "When you have eaten your fill, be sure to praise the Lord your God for the good land he has given you" (Deuteronomy 8:10 NLT).

29. Principle of wise planning

- "A sensible man watches for problems ahead and prepares to meet them. The simpleton never looks, and suffers the consequences" (Proverbs 27:12 TLB).

- "Take a lesson from the ants, you lazybones. Learn from their ways and become wise! Though they have no prince or governor or ruler to make them work, they labor hard all summer, gathering food for the winter. But you, lazybones, how long will you sleep? When will you wake up? A little extra sleep, a little more slumber, a little folding of the hands to rest—then poverty will pounce on you like a bandit; scarcity will attack you like an armed robber" (Proverbs 6:6–11 NLT).

- "But don't begin until you count the cost. For who would begin construction of a building without first calculating the cost to see if there is enough money to finish it? Otherwise, you might complete only the foundation before running out of money, and then everyone would laugh at you" (Luke 14:28–29 NLT).

- "The wise man looks ahead. The fool attempts to fool himself and won't face facts" (Proverbs 14:8 TLB).

30. Principle of wisdom

   - "How much better to get wisdom than gold, and good judgment than silver!" (Proverbs 16:16 NLT).

LIST #38
161 Who's Who Women

Listed from A to Z, here you'll find 161 Bible women and the meaning behind their names.

1. Abigail #1
Meaning: Cause for joy
Scripture: 1 Samuel 25:1–42; 2 Samuel 3:3

Abigail was an intelligent and beautiful woman who saved David from bloodshed by her good judgment and obvious loyalty to him. She put her life at risk to save the men of Nabal's household, and she did save them. David married Abigail and made her his second wife, and she bore David a son named Kileab.

2. Abigail #2
Meaning: Cause for joy
Scripture: 2 Samuel 17:25; 1 Chronicles 2:16–17

Abigail was the sister of Zeruiah and King David and was the daughter of Jesse and Nahash. She was also the wife of Jether and the mother of Amasa, the nephew of King David.

3. Abihail #1
Meaning: Cause of strength; father of splendor
Scripture: 1 Chronicles 2:29

Abihail was the wife of Abishur and the mother of Ahban and Molid.

4. Abihail #2
Meaning: Cause of strength; father of splendor
Scripture: 2 Chronicles 11:18

Abihail was married to David's son Jerimoth. She was the daughter of Jesse's son Eliab and the mother of Mahalath, who married Rehoboam.

5. Abijah
Meaning: My father is Jehovah
Scripture: 2 Kings 18:2; 2 Chronicles 29:1

Abijah was the daughter of Zechariah and the mother of King Hezekiah.

6. Abishag
**Meaning: My father wanders; my father causes
  wandering**
Scripture: 1 Kings 1:3–4; 2:13–25

King David's servants searched throughout Israel for a young, beautiful virgin to care for him in his old age. One of her jobs would be to lie beside him to keep him warm. They chose Abishag, a Shunammite. David was not intimate with her. This had something to do with Adonijah's request to be given Abishag as his wife after David's death. King Solomon ended up putting his brother Adonijah to death for requesting to marry Abishag.

7. Abital
Meaning: Whose father is as dew
Scripture: 2 Samuel 3:4; 1 Chronicles 3:3

Abital bore David his fifth son in Hebron; his name was Shephatiah.

8. Acsah
Meaning: Adorned; bursting the veil
Scripture: Joshua 15:16–17; Judges 1:12–15;
1 Chronicles 2:49

Acsah was the daughter of Caleb. She was given to Othniel, son of Kenaz, Caleb's brother, in marriage as a reward for his attacking and capturing Kiriath Sepher. She urged Othniel to ask her father for a field, but instead, Acsah ended up asking her father Caleb for a special favor. She boldly asked him to give her springs of water, and he granted her request, giving her the upper and lower springs.

9. Adah #1
Meaning: Adornment; beauty; pleasure
Scripture: Genesis 4:19–23

Adah was one of two women married to Lamech. She gave birth to a son named Jabal, who was the father of those who live in tents and raise livestock, and Jubal, who was the father of all who play the harp and flute.

10. Adah #2
Meaning: Adornment; beauty; pleasure
Scripture: Genesis 36:1–16

Adah, a woman of Canaan, was one of Esau's wives. She was the daughter of Elon the Hittite; the mother of Eliphaz; and the grandmother of Teman, Omar, Zepho, Gatam, Kenaz, and Amalek.

11. Ahinoam #1
Meaning: Brother of pleasantries
Scripture: 1 Samuel 14:50

Ahinoam was King Saul's wife, and hers is the only reference to a wife of King Saul. She was also the daughter of Ahimaaz.

12. Ahinoam #2
Meaning: Brother of pleasantries
Scripture: 1 Samuel 25:43; 27:3; 30:5; 2 Samuel 2:2; 3:2;
   1 Chronicles 3:1

Ahinoam of Jezreel was King David's wife and mother of his first son, Amnon. She, along with David's wife Abigail, was captured and taken captive by the Amalekites.

13. Ahlai
Meaning: O would that!
Scripture: 1 Chronicles 2:31, 34–35

Ahlai was the daughter of Sheshan. Her father had only daughters, no sons. Ahlai was given to her father's Egyptian servant Jarha in marriage, and she bore him a son named Attai.

14. Anah
Meaning: (unknown)
Scripture: Genesis 36:2, 14, 18, 25

Anah was the daughter of Zibeon the Hivite. Anah's son was Dishon, and her daughter was Oholibamah.

15. Anna
Meaning: Favor; grace
Scripture: Luke 2:36–38

Anna the prophetess was the daughter of Phanuel of the tribe of Asher. When Jesus was born, she was very old. She had lived with her husband for seven years of marriage; at the age of eighty-four she was still living as a widow. She never left the temple, worshiping night and day with prayer and fasting. Anna approached Mary and Joseph when they brought Jesus to the temple to present him to God according to the Law. Seeing Jesus, she gave thanks to God and spoke about the child to all who were looking forward to the redemption of Jerusalem.

16. Apphia
Meaning: That which is fruitful
Scripture: Philemon 2

Scholars believe that Apphia was probably Philemon's wife. When Paul wrote his letter to Philemon, he referred to Apphia as "our sister."

17. Asenath
Meaning: One who belongs to Neit (the Egyptian goddess of wisdom)
Scripture: Genesis 41:45–50; 46:20

Asenath, daughter of Potiphera, priest of On, was given to Joseph as his wife by Pharaoh. She bore Joseph two sons, Manasseh and Ephraim.

18. Atarah
Meaning: Crown
Scripture: 1 Chronicles 2:26

Atarah was the wife of Jerahmeel and the mother of Onam.

19. Athaliah
Meaning: Taken away of the Lord; Jehovah has afflicted
Scripture: 2 Kings 8:26; 11:1–21; 2 Chronicles 22:1–12; 23:1–21; 24:7

Athaliah was the mother of King Ahaziah and granddaughter of Omri. One of the great influences of the dynasty of Omri in Judah was the power of Athaliah. Athaliah encouraged her son Ahaziah in doing evil. When Ahaziah died, Athaliah murdered the royal family of the house of Judah. She ruled the land for six years, unaware that her grandson Joash had been hidden to keep her from murdering him. One day Athaliah heard the noise of people cheering and realized Joash had been crowned the new king. She tore her robes and shouted, "Treason! Treason!" The troops seized her at the entrance to the Horse Gate on the palace grounds and put her to death.

20. Azubah #1
Meaning: Deserted; desolation
Scripture: 1 Chronicles 2:18–19

Azubah was the wife of Caleb and the mother of three sons, Jesher, Shobab, and Ardon.

21. Azubah #2
Meaning: Deserted; desolation
Scripture: 1 Kings 22:42; 2 Chronicles 20:31

Azubah was the mother of King Jehoshaphat and the daughter of Shilhi.

22. Baara
Meaning: The burning one
Scripture: 1 Chronicles 8:8

Baara was one of two wives Shaharaim divorced.

23. Basemath #1
Meaning: Fragrant; perfumed
Scripture: Genesis 26:34

Basemath, daughter of Elon the Hittite, was one of Esau's wives. Esau's pagan wives, including Basemath, were a source of grief to Esau's parents, Isaac and Rebekah.

24. Basemath #2
Meaning: Fragrant; perfumed
Scripture: Genesis 36:3–4, 10, 13, 17

Basemath (also called Mahalath in Genesis 28:9) was a daughter of Ishmael and sister of Nebaioth, and she was one of Esau's wives. She gave birth to a son named Reuel. Basemath's grandsons were chiefs: Nahath, Zerah, Shammah, and Mizzah.

25. Basemath #3
Meaning: Fragrant; perfumed
Scripture: 1 Kings 4:15

Basemath, daughter of Solomon, was married to Ahimaaz.

26. Bathsheba
Meaning: Seventh daughter; daughter of the oath
Scripture: 2 Samuel 11:2–27; 12:14–15, 24; 1 Kings 1:11–31; 2:13–19; 1 Chronicles 3:5

Bathsheba was a beautiful woman. She was the wife of one of David's mighty men, Uriah the Hittite. Bathsheba slept with David and became pregnant, and David had Uriah killed in battle. After Bathsheba's period of mourning was over, David married her. The son born of their adultery died shortly after birth, but they soon had another son named Solomon, whom, the Bible notes, the Lord loved and nicknamed Jedidiah, meaning "loved by the Lord." David and Bathsheba had three more sons: Shammua, Shobab, and Nathan. Bathsheba fought hard to get Solomon his rightful place on the throne. King David had sworn that Solomon would be the next king after his death, and when Bathsheba reminded him of his oath, he made good on the promise.

27. Bilhah
Meaning: (unknown)
Scripture: Genesis 29:29; 30:3–7; 35:22, 25; 37:2; 46:25; 1 Chronicles 7:13

Laban gave his servant girl Bilhah to his daughter Rachel as a maidservant. Rachel was unable to conceive, so she gave Bilhah to Jacob as a wife. Bilhah became pregnant and gave birth to a son named Dan. She later bore Jacob a second son, Naphtali. After Rachel's death, Jacob's son Reuben slept with Bilhah.

28. Bithiah
Meaning: Daughter of Jehovah
Scripture: 1 Chronicles 4:17–18

Bithiah was an Egyptian princess, a daughter of Pharaoh and the wife of Mered. The meaning of her name suggests she became a worshiper of God. She gave birth to Miriam, Shammai, and Ishbah (the father of Eshtemoa).

29. Candace
Meaning: Queen; ruler of children
Scripture: Acts 8:27

Candace was queen of the Ethiopians. Ethiopian queens were responsible for performing the secular duties of the reigning kings, who were thought to be too sacred for such activities.

30. Chloe
Meaning: Green herb
Scripture: 1 Corinthians 1:10–11

Someone from Chloe's household informed Paul that there had been quarrels among the believers in the Corinthian church.

31. Claudia
Meaning: Lame
Scripture: 2 Timothy 4:21

Claudia was one of the Christians (along with Pudens, Linus, and all the brothers) from whom Paul passed along greetings to Timothy.

32. Cozbi
Meaning: Deceiver; deception
Scripture: Numbers 25:6–18

Cozbi was a Midianite woman, the daughter of Zur, a Midianite tribal chief. She was the lover of an Israelite man named Zimri. Cozbi and Zimri were killed by Phinehas the priest, who drove a spear through both of them to stop a plague that had broken out in the Israelite camp because of the men's immorality with Midianite women.

33. Damaris
Meaning: Heifer
Scripture: Acts 17:34

Damaris was a woman who became a believer after the apostle Paul spoke at the Areopagus in Athens. Some have suggested that she must have been an educated foreigner to have been present at a public meeting there. She might have also been a God-fearing Gentile who heard Paul preach at the synagogue.

34. Deborah #1
Meaning: Bee
Scripture: Genesis 24:59; 35:8

Deborah was Rebekah's nurse who went with her to meet Isaac. After long years of faithful service, Deborah died and was buried under the oak below Bethel. It was named Allon Bacuth, meaning "oak of weeping."

35. Deborah #2
Meaning: Bee
Scripture: Judges 4–5; Hebrews 11:32–34

Deborah was a prophetess who led Israel. She is the only judge said to have been a prophet. The Israelites went to her to have their disputes decided. Her husband was Lappidoth.

"One day she sent for Barak son of Abinoam, who lived in Kedesh in the land of Naphtali. She said to him, 'This is what the Lord, the God of Israel, commands you: Call out 10,000 warriors from the tribes of Naphtali and Zebulun at Mount Tabor. And I will call out Sisera, commander of Jabin's army, along with his chariots and warriors, to the Kishon River. There I will give you victory over him'" (Judges 4:6–7 NLT).

But Barak wouldn't go unless Deborah went with him. She agreed to go but told him that the Lord would hand their enemy, Sisera, over to a woman. As Deborah had said, Sisera was killed by a woman (Jael), and Deborah and Barak sang a song of celebration (the song of Deborah) for their great victory.

36. Delilah
Meaning: Delicate; dainty one
Scripture: Judges 16:4–21

Delilah was the focus of Samson's affection. Philistine rulers bribed her to lure Samson into showing her the secret of his great strength so they could overpower him and tie him up and subdue him. Each promised to pay her eleven hundred shekels of silver to find out his secret.

Three times Delilah asked Samson to tell her the secret of his great strength, and three times he told her something that wasn't true. She nagged him day after day until he gave in and told her the truth. Delilah sent word to the rulers of the Philistines. She then put Samson to sleep on her lap and called a man to shave off the seven braids of his hair. Then she called out to Samson that the Philistines had come for him, but his strength was gone, and the Philistines seized him.

37. Dinah
Meaning: Justice; one who judges
Scripture: Genesis 30:21; 34:1–31

Dinah was the daughter of Jacob and Leah and the sister of Reuben, Simeon, Levi, Judah, Issachar, and Zebulun. One day she was raped by Shechem, son of the Hivite ruler of that area. Shechem claimed he loved Dinah and wanted to marry her. But two of Dinah's brothers, Simeon and Levi, tricked Shechem's family and community when they came to negotiate a bride price. They killed every male in the city.

38. Dorcas
Meaning: Gazelle
Scripture: Acts 9:36–43

Dorcas was the Greek name of a disciple in Joppa; her name in Aramaic was Tabitha. She was the woman Peter raised from the dead.

Dorcas was always doing good and helping the poor. She made robes and other clothing for many people. When she became sick and died, her body was washed and placed in an upstairs room. Some believers sent for Peter, who sent the mourners out of the room and, turning toward the dead woman, said, "Tabitha, get up"—and she did. Many people believed in the Lord because of this miracle.

39. Drusilla
Meaning: Watered by the dew
Scripture: Acts 24:24

Drusilla was a Jewess and the daughter of Herod Agrippa I. According to history, she was married at the age of fifteen to King Azizus but deserted him a year later for Felix, governor of Judea. She had a son named Agrippa who died in the eruption of Vesuvius. Drusilla listened with Felix as Paul spoke about faith in Jesus Christ.

40. Eglah
Meaning: Heifer; chariot
Scripture: 2 Samuel 3:5; 1 Chronicles 3:3

Eglah's husband was King David. Her son, born to David while he was king in Hebron, was Ithream.

41. Elisheba
Meaning: God's oath; God is her oath
Scripture: Exodus 6:23

Elisheba was the daughter of Amminadab and the sister of Nahshon. She married Aaron and gave birth to Nadab, Abihu, Eleazar, and Ithamar.

42. Elizabeth
Meaning: God is my oath
Scripture: Luke 1:5–80

Elizabeth was a descendant of Aaron and the wife of Zechariah the priest. She was upright in God's sight, observing all the Lord's commandments and regulations blamelessly. Elizabeth was well along in years when an angel told Zechariah that Elizabeth would bear him a son, who should be called John. Although Elizabeth had been barren, the angel's words came true. She became pregnant and spent five months in seclusion.

Her relative Mary visited Elizabeth, and at the sound of Mary's greeting, the baby in Elizabeth's womb leaped with joy, and she was filled with the Holy Spirit. Elizabeth told Mary, "You are blessed because you believed that the Lord would do what he said" (Luke 1:45 NLT).

43. Ephah
Meaning: Darkness
Scripture: 1 Chronicles 2:46

Ephah was Caleb's concubine. With Caleb she had two sons: Haran and Moza. The father of Ephah's son Gazez was Haran.

44. Ephrath, Ephrathah
Meaning: Fruitful land
Scripture: 1 Chronicles 2:19, 50; 4:4

Ephrath married Caleb after his wife Azubah died. Hur was the first son born of this union.

45. Esther (Hadassah)
Meaning: Star of hope; fortune; star of joy
Scripture: The book of Esther

Hadassah, who was also known as Esther, was lovely in form and features. She was raised by her cousin Mordecai after her father and mother died. Esther was one of many girls brought to King Xerxes's palace so he could choose a new queen. Esther won the favor of everyone who saw her. Because the king was attracted to Esther more than to any of the other women, he set the royal crown on her head and made her queen.

One day Queen Esther relayed from Mordecai to the king information about an assassination plot and thus saved the king's life. Esther later was encouraged by Mordecai to tell the king about Haman's plan to kill the Jews. She approached the King's throne in hopes of saving her people's lives, but because she came to the throne room without being invited, it could have meant her death. Esther was courageous and willing to die for her people. She petitioned for her life and her people's lives by asking the king to spare them. Xerxes granted her request, and Haman and his ten sons were hanged on the gallows they had prepared for Mordecai.

46. Eunice
Meaning: Conquering well; happy in victory
Scripture: Acts 16:1–3; 2 Timothy 1:5; 3:14–15

Eunice was a believer known for her sincere faith. She was the mother of Paul's protégé Timothy. Several times Paul referred to the strong faith of Timothy's mother, Eunice, and grandmother Lois. He said that from infancy Timothy had known the Scriptures and been convinced of it all because he was taught by his mother at a young age.

47. Euodia
Meaning: Prosperous journey
Scripture: Philippians 4:2–3

Paul mentioned Euodia in the context of her disagreement with another woman, Syntyche. Paul said the feuding women had contended at his side for the gospel, and he pleaded with them to agree in the Lord.

48. Eve
Meaning: Woman; life-giving; mother of all who have life
Scripture: Genesis 2–3; 4:1–2, 25; 2 Corinthians 11:3;
**   1 Timothy 2:13**

God made Eve from Adam's rib so the first man would not be alone. She was called "woman" because she was "taken out of man." Adam named her Eve because "she would become the mother of all the living."

God told Adam and Eve not to eat from the tree in the middle of the Garden, but the cunning serpent persuaded Eve that if she ate the fruit, she would become wise like God. She ate from the tree and gave some of the fruit to her husband, who ate as well. Then their eyes were opened, and they realized they were naked. They hid from God, who punished the pair for their disobedience. Adam and Eve were banished from the Garden of Eden forever.

Although it seems obvious that Eve was the mother of many children (we're not told how long Eve lived, but Adam lived 930 years), the Bible tells us of two of Adam and Eve's sons, Cain and Abel. After Cain killed Abel, Adam and Eve named a new son Seth. "Adam had sexual relations with his wife again, and she gave birth to another son. She named him Seth, for she said, 'God has granted me another son in place of Abel, whom Cain killed'" (Genesis 4:25 NLT).

49. Gomer
Meaning: Completion
Scripture: Hosea 1:1–11; 3:1–5

Gomer was the daughter of Diblaim. Although it seems Gomer was already known for her sexual infidelities, God told the prophet Hosea to marry the unfaithful woman as an object lesson of God's constant love for Israel, a nation that was unfaithful to him.

Gomer gave birth to three children: a son named Jezreel (meaning "God scatters"), a daughter named Lo-Ruhamah (meaning "not loved"), and another son named Lo-Ammi (meaning "not my people"). It's possible Hosea was not the father of Gomer's last two children.

At some point Gomer became a slave. At God's direction Hosea bought her back for fifteen shekels of silver—half the usual price for a slave—and some barley. Though the unfaithful adulteress was being loved by another, Hosea took her back and showed love to her again.

50. Hadassah (see Esther)

51. Hagar
Meaning: Flight; fugitive; immigrant
Scripture: Genesis 16:1–16; 21:9–21; 25:12;
   Galatians 4:21–25

Hagar was Sarah's Egyptian maidservant. Sarah was barren, so she gave Hagar to her husband for a wife. When Hagar knew she was pregnant with Abraham's child, she began to despise her mistress, so Sarah started mistreating her. Hagar fled from Sarah into the wilderness. The angel of the Lord found Hagar and told her to go back and submit to Sarah, promising to bless her and increase her descendants. The angel told Hagar she would have a son, whose name would be Ishmael.

After her son, Isaac, was born, Sarah insisted that Hagar and Ishmael be sent away. They wandered in the desert, but the Lord protected and provided for them. In Galatians 4 Paul used Hagar as a symbol of the old covenant and those who are enslaved to the law as opposed to children of the promise.

52. Haggith
Meaning: Festival; dancer
Scripture: 2 Samuel 3:4–5; 1 Kings 1:5, 11; 2:13;
   1 Chronicles 3:2

Haggith was a wife of King David. While David ruled from Hebron, she gave birth to his fourth son, Adonijah, who later briefly claimed the throne in David's old age.

53. Hammoleketh
Meaning: Queen; regent
Scripture: 1 Chronicles 7:17–18

Hammoleketh was Gilead's sister, Makir's daughter, and Manasseh's granddaughter. She gave birth to Ishhod, Abiezer, and Mahlah. Gideon was also a descendant of Hammoleketh.

54. Hamutal
Meaning: Kinsman of the dew
Scripture: 2 Kings 23:31; 24:18; Jeremiah 52:1

Hamutal was the wife of one king, Josiah, and the mother of two kings: Jehoahaz and Zedekiah. She was from Libnah and was the daughter of Jeremiah.

55. Hannah
Meaning: Gracious; favor
Scripture: 1 Samuel 1:1–28; 2:1–11, 18–21

Hannah was one of Elkanah's two wives. She had not given birth to any children, but Elkanah's other wife, Peninnah, had. Hannah's husband loved her dearly, but Peninnah provoked and irritated Hannah about having no children, causing her much grief through the years. In the temple of the Lord at Shiloh, Hannah wept bitterly and prayed to the Lord. She made a vow that if God would give her a son, she would give him back to the Lord for all the days of his life and that no razor would ever be used on his head (a symbol of devotion to God as a Nazarite).

The Lord answered Hannah's prayer. She conceived and gave birth to a son, Samuel. After she had weaned Samuel, she took him to the temple and gave him to the Lord (to serve in the temple) for his whole life.

The Lord gave Hannah more children to take the place of the one she gave to the Lord. She gave birth to three more sons and two daughters.

56. Hazzelelponi
Meaning: Deliver me, O God who regards me
Scripture: 1 Chronicles 4:3

Hazzelelponi was the daughter of Etam and the sister of Jezreel, Ishma, and Idbash.

57. Helah
Meaning: Sick
Scripture: 1 Chronicles 4:5, 7–8

Helah was one of Ashhur's two wives. She gave birth to four sons: Zereth, Zohar, Ethnan, and Koz.

58. Hephzibah
Meaning: My delight is in her
Scripture: 2 Kings 21:1

Hephzibah was the mother of King Manasseh and wife of King Hezekiah.

59. Herodias
Meaning: Heroic
Scripture: Matthew 14:3–12; Mark 6:14–29; Luke 3:19–20

Herodias was the daughter of Aristobulus and Bernice. She was first married to Herod Philip (by whom she had a daughter), but she left him to marry Philip's more powerful half-brother, Herod Antipas. John the Baptist became Herodias's enemy and was imprisoned for speaking out against Herod's marriage to her.

When Herod Antipas, to reward Herodias's daughter for her pleasing dance on his birthday, promised to give her anything she requested, Herodias prompted her daughter to ask for John the Baptist's head on a platter. The request was granted, and John's head was brought on a platter to the girl, who carried it to her mother.

60. Hodesh
Meaning: New moon
Scripture: 1 Chronicles 8:8–9

Hodesh married Shaharaim after he divorced his wives Hushim and Baara. She gave birth to seven sons: Jobab, Zibia, Mesha, Malcam, Jeuz, Sakia, and Mirmah.

61. Hoglah
Meaning: partridge; boxer
Scripture: Numbers 26:33; 27:1–11; 36:1–12; Joshua 17:1–6

Hoglah was the daughter of Zelophehad, who had five daughters and no sons. Her sisters were Mahlah, Noah, Milcah, and Tirzah. After their father's death, Hoglah and her sisters fought for the right to inherit their father's property. The Lord told Moses that Zelophehad's daughters were right, that they should be given property as an inheritance among their father's relatives, since there were no sons.

Hoglah and her sisters were commanded by the Lord through Moses to marry within their father's tribal clan to ensure the land would not be lost to the clan forever. They did as the Lord commanded and married cousins on their father's side.

62. Huldah
Meaning: Weasel
Scripture: 2 Kings 22:14–20; 2 Chronicles 34:22–33

Huldah the prophetess was married to Shallum, keeper of the wardrobe in King Josiah's court. She lived in Jerusalem's Second District. When the Book of the Law was found during repairs on the temple, Josiah sent representatives to Huldah (even though Jeremiah was also a prophet at that time) to inquire of the Lord about what had been written in the book. She gave them a message from the Lord: what was written in the book was true—God was going to bring disaster on Jerusalem and its people because they had forsaken God and worshiped idols. But the good news was that because Josiah had humbled himself in sorrowful repentance, God would delay his judgment. Huldah promised that Josiah would be buried in peace, without seeing the disaster God would bring upon the land.

63. Hushim
Meaning: To hasten
Scripture: 1 Chronicles 8:8, 11

Hushim and her husband, Shaharaim, had two sons, Abitub and Elpaal, before Shaharaim divorced her.

64. Iscah
Meaning: She will look out
Scripture: Genesis 11:29

Iscah's father was Haran, the brother of Abraham. Her sister was Milcah, and her brother was Lot. She probably lived in Ur of the Chaldees.

65. Jael
Meaning: Wild mountain goat
Scripture: Judges 4:17–22; 5:6, 24–27

Jael was the wife of Heber the Kenite. Sisera turned to the Kenites for refuge when he fled Barak and the Israelite army. Jael offered him refuge in her tent, gave him milk to drink, and covered him up. While he slept, Jael drove a tent peg through his temple into the ground, killing him. In the Song of Deborah, Jael is called the most blessed of women.

66. Jecoliah
Meaning: Powerful
Scripture: 2 Kings 15:2; 2 Chronicles 26:3

Jecoliah was from Jerusalem. Her husband was King Amaziah, and her son was King Azariah, whose throne name was Uzziah.

67. Jedidah
Meaning: Darling of Jehovah
Scripture: 2 Kings 22:1

Jedidah was from Bozkath. She was the daughter of Adaiah and the mother of King Josiah.

68. Jehoaddin
Meaning: Jehovah is her ornament
Scripture: 2 Kings 14:2; 2 Chronicles 25:1

Jehoaddin was the mother of King Amaziah. She was from Jerusalem.

69. Jehosheba
Meaning: Jehovah is her oath
Scripture: 2 Kings 11:2; 2 Chronicles 22:11

Jehosheba was the daughter of King Jehoram, the sister of King Ahaziah, and the aunt of King Joash. She was married to the high priest Jehoiada. Jehosheba stole Ahaziah's son Joash away from the royal princes who were about to be murdered. She hid Joash and his nurse in a bedroom so his grandmother Athaliah couldn't kill him. While Athaliah ruled the land for six years, Joash remained hidden with Jehosheba and Jehoiada until Jehoiada orchestrated the boy's rise to the throne.

70. Jemimah
Meaning: Little dove
Scripture: Job 42:14–15

Jemimah was the first daughter born to Job after his time of trial and great loss. She had two sisters, Keziah and Keren-Happuch, and seven brothers. Jemimah and her sisters were the most beautiful women in the land, and Job granted them an inheritance along with their brothers.

71. Jerioth
Meaning: Tent curtains
Scripture: 1 Chronicles 2:18

Jerioth was one of Caleb's wives. We are told they had children, but their names are not given.

72. Jerusha
Meaning: Taken possession of; married
Scripture: 2 Kings 15:33; 2 Chronicles 27:1–2

Jerusha was the mother of King Jotham, the wife of King Uzziah, and the daughter of Zadok.

73. Jezebel #1
Meaning: Chaste; free from carnal connection
Scripture: 1 Kings 16:31; 18:4–19; 19:1–2; 21:5–25;
    2 Kings 9:1–37

Queen Jezebel's name is mentioned seventeen times in the Bible. She married King Ahab and was instrumental in urging him to do evil. Jezebel killed many prophets of the Lord and honored the prophets of Baal and Asherah by feeding them at her table. She plotted to have Naboth falsely accused of blasphemy and executed so she could confiscate his vineyard for the king. Some scholars have suggested Jezebel means "dunghill."

74. Jezebel #2
Meaning: Chaste; free from carnal connection
Scripture: Revelation 2:18–29

In this passage the name Jezebel is used as an epithet for a prominent woman in the congregation of Thyatira who undermined loyalty to God by promoting tolerance toward pagan practices. With her teaching she misled people into sexual immorality and the eating of food sacrificed to idols. God said he would cast her on a bed of suffering and would make those who committed adultery with her suffer intensely unless they repented. He would strike her children dead. Jezebel is symbolically the spiritual mother of all who pursue false doctrines.

75. Joanna
Meaning: Jehovah has shown favor
Scripture: Luke 8:1–3; 23:55–56; 24:1–11

Joanna was the wife of Cuza, the manager of Herod's house-hold. Joanna, along with some other women, had been cured of diseases or delivered of evil spirits. She was helping to support the twelve disciples out of her own means.
Joanna was one of the women who had come with Jesus from Galilee. After he was crucified, Joanna followed Joseph as he laid Jesus's body in the tomb and thus knew its location. Then the women went home to prepare spices and perfume for Jesus's burial, but they rested the next day because it was the Sabbath.

It seems Joanna was one of the women who returned to the garden to discover that the stone had been rolled away and the tomb was empty. She and the others had an encounter with two angels who told them that Jesus was risen. Then they remembered Jesus's words about rising from the dead. Joanna and the other women told the apostles what they had seen and heard, although no one at first believed their report.

76. Jochebed
Meaning: Glory of Jehovah
Scripture: Exodus 2:1–11; 6:20; Numbers 26:59;
    Hebrews 11:23

Jochebed was the wife of Amram. She was also his aunt, the sister of Amram's father. Jochebed and Amram had three children: Miriam, Aaron, and Moses. Concerned about grow-ing Israelite numbers and strength, Pharaoh ordered that every newborn Hebrew boy was to be thrown into the Nile and drowned. But Jochebed did not obey. She saw that Moses was no ordinary child, so she hid the baby for three months. When she could no longer hide him, she put him in a basket and placed him among the reeds along the bank of the Nile.

Pharaoh's daughter found Moses and felt sorry for the crying baby. Jochebed was allowed to nurse the child until he was older, when she returned him to Pharaoh's daughter, who raised him as her son.

77. Judith
Meaning: The praised one
Scripture: Genesis 26:34

Judith was the daughter of Beeri the Hittite and was one of Esau's wives.

78. Julia
Meaning: Having curly hair
Scripture: Romans 16:15

Julia is mentioned as a saint. She cannot be further identified except that she was part of the church at Rome.

79. Keren-Happuch
Meaning: Beautifier; horn of paint; highly prized
   eyeshadow
Scripture: Job 42:14–15

Keren-Happuch was the third daughter born to Job after his time of great testing and loss. She had two sisters, Jemimah and Keziah, and seven brothers. Keren-Happuch and her sisters were the most beautiful women in the land, and Job granted them an inheritance along with their brothers.

80. Keturah
Meaning: Incense
Scripture: Genesis 25:1–6; 1 Chronicles 1:31–33

Keturah became Abraham's wife after the death of Sarah. Her children with Abraham include Zimran, Jokshan, Medan, Midian, Ishbak, and Shuah.

81. Keziah
Meaning: Cassia; cinnamon
Scripture: Job 42:14–15

Keziah was the second daughter born to Job after his time of great testing and loss. She had two sisters, Jemimah and Keren-Happuch, and seven brothers. Keziah and her sisters were the most beautiful women in the land, and Job granted them an inheritance along with their brothers.

82. Leah
Meaning: Wearied; faint from sickness
Scripture: Genesis 29:16–31:33; 34:1; 35:23; 49:29–31;
   Ruth 4:11

Leah was the older daughter of Laban, and she was Jacob and Esau's cousin. Although Jacob loved Rachel, Laban tricked him into marrying Leah first. In various translations, Leah's eyes are described as "weak" (NIV), "tender" (KJV), or "pretty" (NLT), but Rachel was beautiful in every way. Jacob married Rachel after being married to Leah one week, leading to a bitter rivalry between the sisters. They competed for their husband's love through their children. Leah had six sons: Reuben, Simeon, Levi, Judah, Issachar, and Zebulun. She also had one daughter, Dinah.

When Leah died, she was buried in the cave in the field of Machpelah near Mamre in Canaan. She was buried with Abraham and Sarah and Isaac and Rebekah.

83. Lois
Meaning: Agreeable; desirable
Scripture: 2 Timothy 1:5

Lois was the mother of Eunice and grandmother of Timothy. She was known for her sincere faith that had influenced her children and grandchildren.

84. Lo-Ruhamah
Meaning: Not pitied; not loved
Scripture: Hosea 1:6, 8; 2:1, 23

Lo-Ruhamah was the daughter of the prophet Hosea and his adulterous wife, Gomer. Her name was given to symbolize that God had reached the end of his patience and mercy toward his unfaithful people. However, as seen in Hosea 2:1, 23, the child became Ruhamma, "pitied" or "loved," and her brother Lo-ammi ("not my people") became Ammi ("my loved one"), symbolizing that God would once again love and pity the faithful remnant of his people.

85. Lydia
Meaning: Bending
Scripture: Acts 16:12–15, 40

Lydia was a Gentile businesswoman from the city of Thyatira who dealt in purple cloth. She was a worshiper of God, which meant she believed in the true God and followed the teachings of Scripture but was not a full convert to Judaism. When Paul visited Philippi, he encountered Lydia and a group of women meeting outside the city, near a river, for prayer. (It seems there were not enough Jewish men in Philippi to establish a synagogue.) When Paul spoke to them about Jesus, Lydia became a Christian. She and the members of her home were baptized, and she persuaded Paul and the others to stay at her house.

After Paul and Silas were released from the Philippian prison, they returned to Lydia's house to meet with and encourage the Christians.

86. Maacah #1
Meaning: Oppression; depression
Scripture: 1 Chronicles 2:48–49

Maacah was Caleb's concubine. She gave birth to five sons, Sheber, Tirhanah, Shaaph, Sheva, and Gibea, and one daughter, Acsah.

87. Maacah #2
Meaning: Oppression; depression
Scripture: 1 Chronicles 7:15–16

Maacah was a descendant of the Huppites and Shuppites. She was the wife of Makir and bore him two sons, Peresh and Sheresh. It's not clear if Makir also had a sister named Maacah or if this is the same woman.

88. Maacah #3
Meaning: Oppression; depression
Scripture: 1 Chronicles 8:29–33; 9:35

Maacah was the wife of Jeiel, who was the "father" or founder of the settlement of Gibeon. Maacah and Jeiel had ten sons: Abdon (the firstborn), Zur, Kish, Baal, Ner, Nadab, Gedor, Ahio, Zeker, and Mikloth. Maacah's great-grandson was King Saul.

89. Maacah #4
Meaning: Oppression; depression
Scripture: 1 Chronicles 3:2; 2 Samuel 3:3

Maacah was the daughter of Talmai, king of Geshur. With King David she had a son named Absalom.

90. Maacah #5
Meaning: Oppression; depression
Scripture: 2 Chronicles 13:2; 1 Kings 15:1–2;
  2 Chronicles 11:20–22; 1 Kings 15:10–13;
  2 Chronicles 15:16

Maacah was the wife of King Rehoboam. She was the daughter of Uriel of Gibeah and the granddaughter of King David's son Absalom. Maacah and Rehoboam had sons: Abijah, Attai, Ziza, and Shelomith. Rehoboam loved Maacah more than any of his other wives or concubines and appointed her son, Abijah, to be the chief prince among his brothers and to be the future king.

Maacah was later deposed of her position as queen mother by her grandson, King Asa, for making a repulsive Asherah pole. It might appear that her idolatry was a deliberate attempt to counter Asa's religious reform.

91. Mahlah #1
Meaning: Sickness; disease
Scripture: 1 Chronicles 7:18

Mahlah was the daughter of Hammoleketh and the sister of Ishod and Abiezer.

92. Mahlah #2
Meaning: Sickness; disease
Scripture: Numbers 26:33; 27:1–11; 36:1–12; Joshua 17:3

Mahlah was the oldest daughter of Zelophehad, who had five daughters and no sons. Her sisters were Noah, Mahlah, Milcah, and Tirzah. After their father's death, Hoglah and her sisters fought for the right to inherit their father's property. The Lord told Moses that Zelophehad's daughters were right, that they should be given property as an inheritance among their father's relatives, since there were no sons.

Mahlah and her sisters were commanded by the Lord through Moses to marry within their father's tribal clan to ensure the land would not be lost to the clan forever. They did as the Lord commanded and married cousins on their father's side.

93. Mahalath #1
Meaning: Sickness; disease
Scripture: Genesis 28:9

Mahalath was one of the wives of Esau. She was also the daughter of Ishmael and the sister of Nebaioth.

94. Mahalath #2
Meaning: Sickness; disease
Scripture: 2 Chronicles 11:18–19

Mahalath was the daughter of King David's son Jerimoth and of Abihail, the daughter of Jesse's son Eliab. She was one of King Rehoboam's cousins and wives and was the mother of his sons Jeush, Shemariah, and Zaham.

95. Mara
Meaning: Bitter
Scripture: Ruth 1:20

Mara's real name was Naomi, but she asked to be called Mara, saying, "The Almighty has made my life very bitter." See Naomi.

96. Martha
Meaning: Lord; master
Scripture: Luke 10:38–42; John 11; 12:1–3

Martha, her sister, Mary, and her brother, Lazarus, were friends of Jesus. They lived in Bethany. Many scholars believe Martha may have been the oldest of the three siblings, based on her actions and attitudes.

Martha appears in three incidents in the Gospels. In Luke 10:38–42 Martha opened her home to Jesus and worked hard at hosting while her sister, Mary, sat at the Lord's feet, listening. Annoyed, Martha asked Jesus to tell Mary to help her, but Jesus gently rebuked her, reminding her that Mary had chosen what was better.

In John 11 Mary and Martha sent word to Jesus that their brother, Lazarus, was sick. By the time Jesus arrived, Lazarus had been dead for four days. Martha went out to meet Jesus and told him, "If you had been here, my brother would not have died. But I know that even now God will give you whatever you ask." A short time later Jesus rewarded Martha's faith: he raised Lazarus from the dead.

In John 12 we are told about another dinner given in Jesus's honor, in which Martha served, Lazarus was among those at the table, and Mary anointed Jesus's feet with expensive perfume.

97. Mary #1 (mother of Jesus)
Meaning: Bitterness; trouble; sorrow
Scripture: Matthew 1–2; 12:46; Luke 1–2; John 2:1–11;
    19:25; Acts 1:14

Mary was the mother of Jesus and a descendant of King David. She was married to Joseph, although she became pregnant by the Holy Spirit while they were only betrothed, not married, and she was still a virgin. When the angel Gabriel announced to Mary that she would be the mother of the Son of God, Mary responded, "I am the Lord's servant. May everything you have said about me come true." And then the angel left her (Luke 1:38 NLT).

Mary was a constant and faithful presence in Jesus's life from his birth, through his ministry, to his crucifixion. The last we read of Mary, she was waiting with the other believers in the Upper Room for the promised coming of the Holy Spirit.

98. Mary #2 (Mary Magdalene)
Meaning: Bitterness; trouble; sorrow
Scripture: Matthew 27:56, 61; 28:1, 4–10; Mark 15:40–41;
Luke 8:1–3; 24:1–11; John 19:25; 20:1–18

Mary Magdalene was one of the devoted women who followed Jesus from Galilee. Luke 8:2 identifies her as one from whom Jesus had driven out seven demons. She watched from a distance as Jesus was crucified and then went to the tomb where Jesus was laid.

Mary was one of the women who returned to the tomb on Easter Sunday to anoint Jesus's body with spices but encountered instead the empty tomb and an angel who told the women that Jesus had risen. Mary was the first to see the resurrected Christ.

99. Mary #3 (from Bethany)
Meaning: Bitterness; trouble; sorrow
Scripture: Mark 14:3–9; Luke 10:38–42; John 11:1–46;
12:1–8

Mary lived in Bethany and was the sister of Martha and Lazarus. She seemed especially devoted to Jesus. The Bible shows us Mary sitting at Jesus's feet listening to him teach (Luke 10:38–42), quickly going to Jesus when told he was calling for her (John 11:29), and anointing Jesus's head and feet with expensive perfume and wiping his feet with her hair (Mark 14:3–9; John 12:3). She was present when Jesus raised her brother, Lazarus, from the dead.

100. Mary #4 (mother of James and Joses)
Meaning: Bitterness; trouble; sorrow
Scripture: Mark 15:40–41

Mary was the mother of James the younger and Joses. She was one of the women who followed Jesus from Galilee, taking care of his needs. She was part of the group of women who were present at Jesus's final events on earth—his crucifixion, burial, and the announcement of his resurrection.

101. Mary #5 (mother of John Mark)
Meaning: Bitterness; trouble; sorrow
Scripture: Acts 12:11–17

Mary was the mother of John Mark. Her home seems to have been a place where Christians gathered and prayed. Peter fled to Mary's house when the angel delivered him from prison.

102. Mary #6 (from Rome)
Meaning: Bitterness; trouble; sorrow
Scripture: Romans 16:6

All that is known about Mary of Rome comes from Romans 16:6. Paul greeted Mary and described her as someone who had worked hard for the Roman believers.

103. Matred
Meaning: Thrusting forward
Scripture: Genesis 36:39; 1 Chronicles 1:50

Matred was the daughter of Me-Zahab and the mother of Mehetabel, who was the wife of King Hadad of Edom.

104. Mehetabel
Meaning: Whom God makes happy
Scripture: Genesis 36:39; 1 Chronicles 1:50

Mehetabel was the daughter of Matred, granddaughter of Me-Zahab, and wife of King Hadad of Edom.

105. Merab
Meaning: Increase; multiplication
Scripture: 1 Samuel 14:49; 18:17–19; 2 Samuel 21:8–9; 1 Chronicles 8:33

Merab was King Saul's older daughter. Her younger sister was Michal; her brothers were Jonathan, Ishvi, Malki-Shua, Abinadab, and Esh-Baal (Ish-Bosheth). Saul offered Merab in marriage to David in exchange for his military service, but he was actually jealously hoping David would die in battle. In humility David declined the honor of marrying the king's daughter, and she married Adriel of Meholah. Years later Merab's five sons were turned over to the Gibeonites along with two other descendants of Saul. They were put to death and their bodies left on a hill.

106. Meshullemeth
Meaning: Those who pay; retribution
Scripture: 2 Kings 21:18–19

Meshullemeth was the mother of Judah's King Amon and the wife of King Manasseh. She was from Jotbah and was the daughter of Haruz.

107. Michal
Meaning: Who is like Jehovah?
Scripture: 1 Samuel 14:49; 18:20–29; 19:11–17; 25:44; 2 Samuel 3:13–16; 6:16–23; 1 Chronicles 8:33; 15:29

Michal was the younger daughter of King Saul. Her older sister was Merab; her brothers were Jonathan, Ishvi, Malki-Shua, Abinadab, and Esh-Baal (Ish-Bosheth). She fell in love with David—a development Saul tried to use to destroy David. Saul offered David the privilege of marrying Michal and becoming the king's son-in-law for a bride price of a hundred Philistine foreskins, hoping the Philistines would kill David. But David won his bride by killing (with the help of his men) two hundred Philistines.

Later Michal warned David that King Saul was trying to kill him and helped him escape. While David was running from Saul's fury, Saul had Michal marry a man from Gallim, Palti, son of Laish. She was then taken away from Palti and returned to David as a condition of his alliance with Abner that eventually made David king over all Israel. Palti followed behind Michal, weeping for losing her.

When Michal saw King David dancing before the Lord, she despised David in her heart. Michal had no children.

108. Milcah #1
Meaning: Queen; counsel
Scripture: Genesis 11:29; 22:20–23; 24:15, 24, 47

Milcah was the daughter of Haran and wife of Haran's brother Nahor. She gave birth to eight sons: Uz, Buz, Kemuel, Kesed, Hazo, Pildash, Jidlaph, and Bethuel. She was the grandmother of Rebekah and Laban.

109. Milcah #2
Meaning: Queen; counsel
Scripture: Numbers 26:33; 27:1–11; 36:1–12; Joshua 17:1–6

Milcah was the daughter of Zelophehad, who had five daughters and no sons. Her sisters were Mahlah, Noah, Hoglah, and Tirzah. After their father's death, Milcah and her sisters fought for the right to inherit their father's property. The Lord told Moses that Zelophehad's daughters were right, that they should be given property as an inheritance among their father's relatives, since there were no sons.

Milcah and her sisters were commanded by the Lord through Moses to marry within their father's tribal clan to ensure the land would not be lost to the clan forever. They did as the Lord commanded and married cousins on their father's side.

110. Miriam #1
Meaning: Bitterness; rebellion
Scripture: Exodus 15:20–21; Numbers 12:1–15; 20:1;
   26:59; Deuteronomy 24:9; 1 Chronicles 6:3;
   Micah 6:4

Miriam was the sister of Aaron and Moses and the daughter of Amram and Jochebed. Although she is not named, she probably was the sister who stood watch over baby Moses's basket when it was placed in the Nile River.

She was described as a prophetess in connection with the celebratory song and dance in which she led Israel after crossing the Red Sea. Miriam assisted Moses in leading the people of Israel in their journey to the Promised Land (Micah 6:4). But when she and Aaron rebelled against God by complaining against Moses, God struck her with leprosy for seven days. She seemed to be the leader in this rebellion, as she was stricken but Aaron was not. Miriam died and was buried at Kadesh, in the desert of Zin.

111. Miriam #2
Meaning: Bitterness; rebellion
Scripture: 1 Chronicles 4:17

One of Mered's wives gave birth to a daughter named Miriam.

112. Naamah #1
Meaning: Pleasant; sweetness
Scripture: Genesis 4:22

Naamah was the daughter of Lamech, a descendant of Cain, and Zillah. Her brother, Tubal-Cain, was the inventor of forged tools.

113. Naamah #2
Meaning: Pleasant; sweetness
Scripture: 1 Kings 14:21, 31; 2 Chronicles 12:13

Naamah was an Ammonite woman, one of King Solomon's many wives. She was the mother of King Rehoboam.

114. Naarah
Meaning: Child of the Lord
Scripture: 1 Chronicles 4:5–6

Naarah was one of the two wives of Ashhur, a descendant of Judah. She was the mother of Ahuzzam, Hepher, Temeni, and Haahashtari.

115. Naomi
Meaning: My joy; my bliss
Scripture: The book of Ruth

Naomi's husband was Elimelech; their sons were Mahlon and Kilion. A famine caused them to leave their home in Bethlehem in Judah and go to Moab. Her husband and both sons died in Moab, so Naomi returned to Judah with her Moabite daughter-in-law Ruth, Mahlon's widow. Naomi was pivotal in arranging a second marriage for Ruth with Boaz, the family's wealthy kinsman-redeemer. When Ruth and Boaz had a son, Obed, Naomi cared for him as if he were her own. Obed was the grandfather of King David.

116. Nehushta
Meaning: A piece of brass
Scripture: 2 Kings 24:8–15

Nehushta was the wife of King Jehoiakim and mother of King Jehoiachin. She was from Jerusalem and was the daughter of Elnathan. After her son had reigned over Jerusalem for just three months, the city was besieged and conquered by Nebuchadnezzar of Babylon. Nehushta accompanied her son to Babylon in captivity, along with the leading people of the land.

117. Noadiah
Meaning: One to whom the Lord revealed himself
Scripture: Nehemiah 6:14

Noadiah was a prophetess who tried to intimidate Nehemiah.

118. Noah
Meaning: Rest; comfort
Scripture: Numbers 26:33; 27:1

Noah was a daughter of Zelophehad, who had five daughters and no sons. Her sisters were Mahlah, Hoglah, Milcah, and Tirzah. After their father's death, Noah and her sisters fought for the right to inherit their father's property. The Lord told Moses that Zelophehad's daughters were right, that they should be given property as an inheritance among their father's relatives, since there were no sons.

Noah and her sisters were commanded by the Lord through Moses to marry within their father's tribal clan to ensure the land would not be lost to the clan forever. They did as the Lord commanded and married cousins on their father's side.

119. Oholibamah
Meaning: Tent of high places
Scripture: Genesis 36:2–25

Oholibamah, daughter of Anah and granddaughter of Zibeon the Hivite, was one of Esau's wives. She bore Esau three sons: Jeush, Jalam, and Korah.

120. Orpah
Meaning: Fawn; young doe
Scripture: Ruth 1

Orpah was a Moabite woman who married one of Naomi's sons. When Naomi started back to Israel after the deaths of her husband and both sons, her sons' widows, Orpah and Ruth, started the journey with her. At Naomi's urging, Orpah turned back to go home to her people, while Ruth steadfastly refused to leave Naomi's side.

121. Peninnah
Meaning: Coral
Scripture: 1 Samuel 1:1–7

Peninnah was one of Elkanah's two wives; Hannah was the other. Peninnah had children, but Hannah had none. Peninnah provoked Hannah as a rival, deliberately trying to irritate her. Eventually Hannah became the mother of Samuel and other children after God answered Hannah's prayer.

122. Persis
Meaning: One who takes by storm
Scripture: Romans 16:12

In the book of Romans, Paul sent greetings to his dear friend Persis, describing her as a woman who had worked hard in the Lord.

123. Phoebe
Meaning: Pure; radiant
Scripture: Romans 16:1–2

Phoebe was a servant or a deaconess of the church in Cenchrea. Paul asked the Roman Christians to receive Phoebe in the Lord in a way worthy of the saints and to give her any help she might need. He complimented her by saying she had been a big help to many people, including himself. It's possible that Phoebe was the person to whom Paul entrusted his letter to be delivered to the church in Rome.

124. Priscilla
Meaning: Worthy; venerable
Scripture: Acts 18:1–4, 18–19, 24–26; Romans 16:3–4;
    1 Corinthians 16:19; 2 Timothy 4:19

Priscilla and her husband, Aquila, had been forced to leave Italy when Emperor Claudius ordered all Jews to leave Rome. Paul stayed and worked with them while in Corinth because they were tentmakers, as he was. Paul and Luke consistently mentioned Priscilla before her husband, which might indicate that she had higher social status or the more dominant personality.

Priscilla and Aquila sailed with Paul for Syria. He left them at Ephesus and continued on. When a man named Apollos came to town preaching about Jesus, but with incomplete knowledge, they invited him to their home and "explained to him the way of God more adequately" (Acts 18:26).

A church met in the couple's home. Paul spoke highly of Priscilla as a fellow worker in Christ Jesus. She risked her life for Paul, and the churches of the Gentiles were grateful to her and her husband.

125. Puah
Meaning: Childbearing; joy of parents
Scripture: Exodus 1:15–21

Puah was a Hebrew midwife in Egypt at the time of Moses's birth. Pharaoh commanded the midwives to kill all the Hebrew boys they delivered. But the midwives feared God and didn't obey Pharaoh.

When Pharaoh summoned them and demanded an explanation for letting the boys live, they told him: "Hebrew women are not like Egyptian women; they are vigorous and give birth before the midwives arrive" (Exodus 1:19). God was kind to the midwives and blessed them with families of their own because they feared God.

126. Rachel
Meaning: Ewe; lamb
Scripture: Genesis 29–31; 33:1, 2, 7; 35:16–26; 48:7;
    Ruth 4:11

Rachel was the most-loved wife of Jacob and was the mother of Joseph and Benjamin. She was a shepherdess, the daughter of Laban, and Jacob's cousin. Her sister was Leah.

Jacob loved Rachel and made a deal to work for her father for seven years in exchange for being allowed to marry her. But at the end of that time, Laban switched daughters, and Jacob found he had married Leah instead. After one week Jacob also married Rachel.

Rachel was beautiful, and Jacob loved her more than he loved Leah. This led to a bitter rivalry between the sisters. They competed for their husband's love through their children. Because Rachel had difficulty conceiving, she gave Jacob her servant, Bilhah, as a wife. Bilhah had two sons, Dan and Naphtali.

When Jacob took his family and fled from Laban, Rachel stole her father's household gods. As they neared Jacob's homeland, Esau and four hundred armed men came to meet them. Jacob divided his family into four groups and put Rachel and Joseph in the back to keep his favorite wife and child far away from potential harm. As Rachel and her family moved from Bethel, Rachel began to give birth and died during that time, before reaching Canaan. She named him Ben-Oni, "son of my trouble," but Jacob renamed him Benjamin, "son of my right hand."

127. Rahab
Meaning: Insolence; fierceness
Scripture: Joshua 2:1–21; 6:17–25; Matthew 1:5;
    Hebrews 11:31; James 2:25

Rahab was called a prostitute, but some sources refer to her as an innkeeper. She hid the two spies Joshua had sent to scout out Jericho. When the king of Jericho sent men looking for the spies, she hid the spies and helped them escape safely. They made a pact that Rahab and her family would be safe when they returned as long as she kept their secret and tied a scarlet cord in the window through which she helped them escape.

When Jericho was conquered, the spies' oath to Rahab was honored, and Rahab and her family became part of the Israelite community. Rahab became the mother of Boaz (Ruth's husband) and ancestor of Jesus. In Hebrews 11:31 and James 2:25, Rahab is used as a symbol for faith and good works.

128. Rebekah
Meaning: Tie a rope for animals; a hitching place
Scripture: Genesis 22:23; 24; 25:20–28; 26:6–35; 27;
   28:1–5; 29:12; 35:8; 49:31

Rebekah was the wife of Isaac and the mother of Jacob and Esau. Her brother was Laban, her father was Bethuel, and her nurse was Deborah. Abraham sent his servant to his homeland to find a wife for his son Isaac. When the servant found Rebekah, she offered to water his camels—a sign the servant had asked God to give to show which woman God had chosen for Isaac. Rebekah agreed to leave immediately to go back with the servant and marry Isaac.

Rebekah was beautiful. Isaac married her and loved her, but she was barren for twenty years. When Isaac prayed, the Lord answered his prayer, and Rebekah became pregnant. When she experienced unusual jostling in her womb, she asked God why this was happening. God responded: "Two nations are in thy womb, and two manner of people shall be separated from thy bowels; and the one people shall be stronger than the other people; and the elder shall serve the younger" (Genesis 25:23 KJV).

Twins were born: Esau, the older, and Jacob. Esau preferred his rugged outdoorsy son, Esau, but Rebekah loved Jacob. When Isaac was blind in his old age, Rebekah masterminded a plan for Jacob to deceive his father into giving him the blessing that normally belonged to the firstborn.

Although Rebekah won the blessing for her favorite son, she lost him as a result: she sent him to her brother Laban in Paddan Aram to escape Esau's murderous fury. By the time he returned with his family many years later, we read no more of Rebekah, and it's presumed that she died without ever seeing Jacob again. She was buried with Isaac in a cave in the field of Machpelah, near Mamre in Canaan.

129. Reumah
Meaning: Exalted
Scripture: Genesis 22:24

Reumah was the concubine of Nahor, the brother of Abraham. She gave birth to four sons: Tebah, Gaham, Tahash, and Maacah.

130. Rhoda
Meaning: Rose
Scripture: Acts 12:1–19

Rhoda was a servant of Mary, the mother of John Mark. When the believers met at the house to pray for Peter, who had been imprisoned for his testimony, it was she who answered his knock on the door and heard his voice. Overjoyed, she ran back to tell the others without opening the door and letting Peter inside.

131. Rizpah
Meaning: Baking stone
Scripture: 2 Samuel 3:7; 21:1–14

Rizpah was the daughter of Aiah and was the concubine of King Saul, by whom she had two sons, Armoni and Mephibosheth. Saul's son Ish-Bosheth accused his powerful general, Abner, of sleeping with Rizpah and feared he was strengthening Abner's own hand to take over the kingdom from the weak Ish-Bosheth. Offended, Abner switched his support to David, who was king at Hebron, leading to Ish-Bosheth's quick demise.

To atone for Saul's killing of the Gibeonites in spite of a peace treaty, the Gibeonites killed and exposed the bodies of Rizpah's two sons, along with five grandsons of Saul. Camping out on sackcloth spread over a rock, Rizpah kept watch over their dead bodies to keep the birds and wild beasts from touching them. She continued her vigil from the beginning of the barley harvest until the late rains. King David took notice of her heroic actions and had the men's bones gathered up and buried honorably in the family tomb.

132. Ruth
Meaning: Something worth seeing
Scripture: The book of Ruth; Matthew 1:5

Ruth was a Moabite woman who married one of Naomi's sons. After the death of her husband, Ruth chose to stay with her mother-in-law and return with her to Israel. Ruth told Naomi, "Intreat me not to leave thee, or to return from following after thee: for whither thou goest, I will go; and where thou lodgest, I will lodge: thy people shall be my people, and thy God my God" (Ruth 1:16 KJV).

In Israel Ruth began gleaning grain in the field of a man named Boaz. Boaz showed favor to Ruth and protected her. Naomi was pivotal in arranging a second marriage for Ruth with Boaz, the family's wealthy kinsman-redeemer. Ruth and Boaz had a son, Obed, who was the grandfather of King David.

133. Salome #1
Meaning: Peace
Scripture: Matthew 14:6–11; Mark 6:22–28

Salome's name is not mentioned in the Gospels, but Josephus recorded her name in his histories. Salome was the daughter of Herodias, the wife of Herod Antipas. Her father was Herod Philip, Herodias's first husband and brother of Herod Antipas. On Herod Antipas's birthday Salome danced for him, and she so pleased him that he promised to give her whatever she asked for. Prompted by her mother, Salome asked for the head of John the Baptist on a platter. John was killed and his head brought to Salome, who carried it to her mother.

134. Salome #2
Meaning: Peace
Scripture: Matthew 20:20–24; 27:56; Mark 15:40–41;
    16:1–8

Salome was one of the women who followed Jesus from Galilee, taking care of his needs. She was part of the group of women who were present at Jesus's final events on earth—his crucifixion, burial, and the announcement of his resurrection. By comparing names in different lists of women at the cross, some scholars have concluded that Salome was likely the wife of Zebedee and the mother of James and John. Some have even deduced from John 19:25 that she was the sister of Jesus's mother, Mary, making her Jesus's aunt and James and John his cousins.

James and John's mother asked the Lord to allow one of her sons to sit on his left and the other on his right in his kingdom. Jesus told her, "You don't know what you are asking" (Matthew 20:22).

135. Sapphira
Meaning: Sapphire
Scripture: Acts 5:1–11

Sapphira was married to Ananias, and both were part of the early church in Jerusalem. Perhaps under self-imposed pressure to keep up with others in the church (such as Barnabas, who sold property and donated the money to the work of the church), Ananias and Sapphira sold some land and laid some of the proceeds at the apostles' feet. They kept part of the money for themselves and lied, saying the portion they had given was the entire amount they had been paid for the land.

Peter confronted first Ananias and later Sapphira about lying to the Holy Spirit. "Why has Satan filled your heart? You lied to the Holy Spirit, and you kept some of the money for yourself. The property was yours to sell or not sell, as you wished. And after selling it, the money was yours to give away. How could you do a thing like this? You weren't lying to us but to God" (Acts 5:3–4 NLT). Sapphira and her husband each fell to the floor dead, and great fear gripped the church and all who heard what had happened.

136. Sarah, Sarai
Meaning: Princess; contentious; quarrelsome
Scripture: Genesis 11:29–31; 12:5–17; 16:1–15; 17:1–22;
    18:1–15; 20:2–18; 21:1–12; 23:1–20

Sarai was the wife and half-sister of Abram. Sarai and Abram left Ur of the Chaldeans with Abram's father, Terah, and nephew, Lot, to go to Canaan. God had promised to make a great nation of Abram, but Abram had no children because Sarai was barren. Growing old without seeing God's promise fulfilled, Sarai concocted a plan for building a family through her Egyptian servant Hagar. Abraham slept with Hagar, who, when she became pregnant, began to despise Sarai, and Sarai mistreated her.

When Sarai was eighty-nine and Abram ninety-nine, God renewed his promise and told Abram that Sarai would indeed have a son. God changed Abram's name to Abraham ("father of many"), and Sarai's to Sarah.

When Sarah, listening in her tent, overheard God saying that he would bless her and give her a son, that she would be the mother of nations and that kings would come from her, she laughed. When the Lord asked her why she laughed, Sarah lied because she was afraid and said she didn't laugh.

God kept his promise, and a year later, at the age of ninety, Sarah gave birth to a baby boy. He was named Isaac, meaning "laughter." Sarah died at the age of 127 in Hebron and was buried in the cave of Machpelah, near Mamre.

137. Serah
Meaning: Abundance
Scripture: Genesis 46:17; Numbers 26:46;
  1 Chronicles 7:30

Serah was the daughter of Asher (son of Jacob and Zilpah). Her four brothers were Imnah, Ishvah, Ishvi, and Beriah.

138. Shelomith #1
Meaning: God is peace; peaceful
Scripture: Leviticus 24:10–15

Shelomith was an Israelite woman, the daughter of Dibri of the tribe of Dan. She was married to an Egyptian man. Their son was stoned to death because he blasphemed God's name.

139. Shelomith #2
Meaning: God is peace; peaceful
Scripture: 1 Chronicles 3:19

Shelomith was the daughter of Zerubbabel. Her two brothers were Meshullam and Hananiah.

140. Sheerah
Meaning: A female relation by blood
Scripture: 1 Chronicles 7:24

Sheerah was the daughter of Ephraim. She built the towns of Lower and Upper Beth Horon as well as Uzzen Sheerah.

141. Shimeath
Meaning: Fame
Scripture: 2 Kings 12:19–21

Shimeath had a son named Jozabad who was one of the officials who murdered King Joash.

142. Shiphrah
Meaning: Prolific; to procreate
Scripture: Exodus 1:15–21

Shiphrah was a Hebrew midwife in Egypt at the time of Moses's birth. Pharaoh commanded the midwives to kill all the Hebrew boys they delivered. But the midwives feared God and didn't obey Pharaoh.

When Pharaoh summoned them and demanded an explanation for letting the boys live, they told him: "Because the Hebrew women are not as the Egyptian women; for they are lively, and are delivered ere the midwives come in unto them" (Exodus 1:19 KJV). God was kind to the midwives and blessed them with families of their own because they feared God.

143. Shomer
Meaning: Keeper; guarded of the Lord
Scripture: 2 Kings 12:21

Shomer had a son named Jehozabad. He was one of the officials who murdered Joash.

144. Susanna
Meaning: White lily
Scripture: Luke 8:1–3

Susanna was one of the women who followed Jesus and contributed from their own resources to support Jesus and his disciples. Jesus may have healed her of some disease or evil spirit (Luke 8:2).

145. Syntyche
Meaning: Fortunate
Scripture: Philippians 4:2–3

Paul mentioned Syntyche in the context of her disagreement with another woman, Euodia. Paul said the feuding women had contended at his side for the gospel, and he pleaded with them to agree in the Lord.

146. Tahpenes
Meaning: The head of the age
Scripture: 1 Kings 11:19–20

Tahpenes was the wife of Pharaoh of Egypt around the time of David and Solomon. Pharaoh showed his approval of Hadad the Edomite by giving him Tahpenes' sister for a wife. Tahpenes' sister had a son, Genubath, who was raised in Pharaoh's palace with the sons of Pharaoh.

147. Tamar #1
Meaning: (unknown)
**Scripture: Genesis 38:6–30; Ruth 4:12; 1 Chronicles
    2:4; Matthew 1:3**

Tamar was the wife of Judah's oldest son, Er, and Judah's second son, Onan. She also gave birth to twins fathered by Judah himself. God put Er to death for his wickedness, so Judah told Onan to marry Tamar and raise a son who would be his brother Er's heir. But Onan was not willing to have a child who would not be his own heir, so he took steps to keep Tamar from getting pregnant. The Lord considered this wicked and took Onan's life too.

At Judah's instructions, Tamar returned home to live with her parents until Judah's youngest son, Shelah, was old enough to marry her. But Judah didn't really want to have his last son marry Tamar for fear he might die too.

In time Tamar realized that Judah was ignoring her, consigning her to a life without prospect of a husband and children, and she took matters into her own hands. After Judah's wife died, Tamar disguised herself as a prostitute and deceived Judah and slept with him. She became pregnant by Judah and had twin boys, Perez and Zerah.

148. Tamar #2
Meaning: (unknown)
Scripture: 2 Samuel 13; 1 Chronicles 3:9

Tamar's father was King David. Her mother was Maacah, daughter of King Talmai of Geshur. Her full brother was Absalom. Tamar's half-brother Amnon fell in love with her and tricked David into sending Tamar to his room by feigning illness. When they were alone, Amnon raped her. Then his passionate love turned to intense hatred, and he further disgraced Tamar by rejecting her. She put ashes on her head, tore her ornamented robe that virgins wore, and went away weeping. She lived in her brother Absalom's home, bitter and desolate. Two years later Absalom took revenge on Amnon, killing him for what he had done to Tamar.

149. Tamar #3
Meaning: (unknown)
Scripture: 2 Samuel 14:27

Tamar was the beautiful daughter of Absalom. He likely named her after his sister. Tamar had three brothers.

150. Taphath
Meaning: A drop of myrrh
Scripture: 1 Kings 4:7, 11

Taphath was the daughter of Solomon and the wife of Ben-Abinadab, one of Solomon's twelve district governors.

151. Timna
Meaning: Restraint
Scripture: Genesis 36:12, 22; 1 Chronicles 1:39

Timna was the concubine of Eliphaz, Esau's son. She and Eliphaz had a son named Amalek. Her brother was Lotan.

152. Tirzah
Meaning: (unknown)
Scripture: Numbers 26:33; 27:1–11; 36:1–12;
    Joshua 17:1–6

Tirzah was the daughter of Zelophehad, who had five daughters and no sons. Her sisters were Mahlah, Noah, Hoglah, and Milcah. After their father's death, Tirzah and her sisters fought for the right to inherit their father's property. The Lord told Moses that Zelophehad's daughters were right, that they should be given property as an inheritance among their father's relatives, since there were no sons.

Tirzah and her sisters were commanded by the Lord through Moses to marry within their father's tribal clan to ensure the land would not be lost to the clan forever. They did as the Lord commanded and married cousins on their father's side.

153. Tryphena and Tryphosa
Meaning: Delicate; dainty one
Scripture: Romans 16:12

Tryphena and Tryphosa were women Paul greeted in his letter to the Roman believers as "women who work hard in the Lord." Because their names are derived from the same Greek root, some have supposed the two were sisters, perhaps even twins.

154. Vashti
Meaning: The once desired; the beloved
Scripture: Esther 1; 2:1, 4, 17

After 187 days of feasting, the Persian king Xerxes ordered Queen Vashti to appear and display her beauty to his guests. She refused to come. Furious, Xerxes consulted with his advisors, who recommended that Vashti never again be allowed to enter the king's presence and that she lose her royal position. Xerxes took their advice and eventually replaced Vashti with Esther.

155. Zebidah
Meaning: Bestowal; gift
Scripture: 2 Kings 23:36

Zebidah was the mother of King Jehoiakim and the wife of King Josiah. She came from Rumah and was the daughter of Pedaiah.

156. Zeresh
Meaning: Star of adoration
Scripture: Esther 5:10–14; 6:12–14

Zeresh was the wife of Haman, who was the enemy of Mordecai and the Jews during the reign of Queen Esther. Zeresh advised Haman to have a seventy-five-foot-tall gallows built on which to hang Mordecai.

157. Zeruah
Meaning: Leprous
Scripture: 1 Kings 11:26

Zeruah was the widow of Nebat and the mother of Jeroboam, the official who rebelled against Kings Solomon and Rehoboam.

158. Zibiah
Meaning: Female gazelle
Scripture: 2 Kings 12:1; 2 Chronicles 24:1

Zibiah, from Beersheba, was the mother of King Joash and the wife of King Ahaziah.

159. Zillah
Meaning: Shadow of darkness; shadow of protection
Scripture: Genesis 4:19–22

Zillah was one of Lamech's two wives. She bore Lamech a son named Tubal-Cain, who forged tools out of bronze and iron.

160. Zilpah
Meaning: (unknown)
Scripture: Genesis 29:24; 30:9–13; 35:26; 37:2; 46:18

Zilpah was Leah's maidservant. When Leah stopped having children, she gave Zilpah to Jacob as a wife. Zilpah gave birth to two sons, Gad and Asher.

161. Zipporah
Meaning: Little bird; sparrow
Scripture: Exodus 2:15–22; 4:24–26; 18:1–6

Zipporah was a shepherdess, the wife of Moses; the mother of Gershom and Eliezer; and a daughter of Reuel (also called Jethro), a priest of Midian. Moses saved Zipporah and her sisters from shepherds who tried to drive them and their flocks away. Then Ziporrah saved Moses's life by circumcising their son Gershom when God was about to kill Moses. It seems Zipporah and her sons stayed with her father, Jethro, while Moses led the Israelites out of Egypt, then met up with Moses in the desert near Mount Horeb.

■ LIST #39
59 Scriptures about Taming the Tongue

James the brother of Jesus wrote that if we can control our tongues, we'll be able to control every other area in our lives. This is an awesome thought. Here's what else the Bible has to say about what *we* say.

1. "Watch over your heart with all diligence, for from it flow the springs of life. Put away from you a deceitful mouth and put devious speech far from you" (Proverbs 4:23–24 NASB).

2. "A worthless person, a wicked man, is the one who walks with a perverse mouth, who winks with his eyes, who signals with his feet, who points with his fingers; who with perversity in his heart continually devises evil, who spreads strife" (Proverbs 6:12–14 NASB).

3. "There are six things which the Lord hates, yes, seven which are an abomination to Him: a false witness who utters lies, and one who spreads strife among brothers" (Proverbs 6:16, 19 NASB).

4. "The mouth of the righteous is a fountain of life, but the mouth of the wicked conceals violence. Hatred stirs up strife, but love covers all transgressions. On the lips of the discerning, wisdom is found, but a rod is for the back of him who lacks understanding. Wise men store up knowledge, but with the mouth of the foolish, ruin is at hand" (Proverbs 10:11–14 NASB).

5. "When there are many words, transgression is unavoidable, but he who restrains his lips is wise. The tongue of the righteous is as choice silver, the heart of the wicked is worth little. The lips of the righteous feed many, but fools die for lack of understanding" (Proverbs 10:19–21 NASB).

6. "The mouth of the righteous flows with wisdom, but the perverted tongue will be cut out. The lips of the righteous bring forth what is acceptable, but the mouth of the wicked what is perverted" (Proverbs 10:31–32 NASB).

7. "With his mouth the godless man destroys his neighbor, but through knowledge the righteous will be delivered" (Proverbs 11:9 NASB).

8. "By the blessing of the upright a city is exalted, but by the mouth of the wicked it is torn down" (Proverbs 11:11 NASB).

9. "He who goes about as a talebearer reveals secrets, but he who is trustworthy conceals a matter" (Proverbs 11:13 NASB).

10. "The words of the wicked lie in wait for blood, but the mouth of the upright will deliver them" (Proverbs 12:6 NASB).

11. "An evil man is ensnared by the transgression of his lips, but the righteous will escape from trouble. A man will be satisfied with good by the fruit of his words, and the deeds of a man's hands will return to him" (Proverbs 12:13–14 NASB).

12. "He who speaks truth tells what is right, but a false witness, deceit. There is one who speaks rashly like

the thrusts of a sword, but the tongue of the wise brings healing. Truthful lips will be established forever, but a lying tongue is only for a moment" (Proverbs 12:17–19 NASB).

13. "Lying lips are an abomination to the LORD, but those who deal faithfully are His delight. A prudent man conceals knowledge, but the heart of fools proclaims folly" (Proverbs 12:22–23 NASB).

14. "Anxiety in a man's heart weighs it down, but a good word makes it glad" (Proverbs 12:25 NASB).

15. "From the fruit of a man's mouth he enjoys good, but the desire of the treacherous is violence. The one who guards his mouth preserves his life; the one who opens wide his lips comes to ruin" (Proverbs 13:2–3 NASB).

16. "In the mouth of the foolish is a rod for his back, but the lips of the wise will protect them" (Proverbs 14:3 NASB).

17. "A trustworthy witness will not lie, but a false witness utters lies" (Proverbs 14:5 NASB).

18. "A truthful witness saves lives, but he who utters lies is treacherous" (Proverbs 14:25 NASB).

19. "A gentle answer turns away wrath, but a harsh word stirs up anger. The tongue of the wise makes knowledge acceptable, but the mouth of fools spouts folly" (Proverbs 15:1–2 NASB).

20. "A soothing tongue is a tree of life, but perversion in it crushes the spirit" (Proverbs 15:4 NASB).

21. "The lips of the wise spread knowledge, but the hearts of fools are not so" (Proverbs 15:7 NASB).

22. "The mind of the intelligent seeks knowledge, but the mouth of fools feeds on folly" (Proverbs 15:14 NASB).

23. "A man has joy in an apt answer, and how delightful is a timely word!" (Proverbs 15:23 NASB).

24. "The heart of the righteous ponders how to answer, but the mouth of the wicked pours out evil things" (Proverbs 15:28 NASB).

25. "A divine decision is in the lips of the king; his mouth should not err in judgment" (Proverbs 16:10 NASB).

26. "Righteous lips are the delight of kings, and he who speaks right is loved" (Proverbs 16:13 NASB).

27. "The heart of the wise instructs his mouth and adds persuasiveness to his lips. Pleasant words are a honeycomb, sweet to the soul and healing to the bones" (Proverbs 16:23–24 NASB).

28. "A worthless man digs up evil, while his words are like scorching fire. A perverse man spreads strife, and a slanderer separates intimate friends" (Proverbs 16:27–28 NASB).

29. "Excellent speech is not fitting for a fool, much less are lying lips to a prince" (Proverbs 17:7 NASB).

30. "He who conceals a transgression seeks love, but he who repeats a matter separates intimate friends. A rebuke goes deeper into one who has understanding than a hundred blows into a fool" (Proverbs 17:9–10 NASB).

31. "He who restrains his words has knowledge, and he who has a cool spirit is a man of understanding. Even a fool, when he keeps silent, is considered wise; when he closes his lips, he is considered prudent" (Proverbs 17:27–28 NASB).

32. "The words of a man's mouth are deep waters; the fountain of wisdom is a bubbling brook" (Proverbs 18:4 NASB).

33. "A fool's lips bring strife, and his mouth calls for blows. A fool's mouth is his ruin, and his lips are the snare of his soul. The words of a whisperer are like dainty morsels, and they go down into the innermost parts of the body" (Proverbs 18:6–8 NASB).

34. "He who gives an answer before he hears, it is folly and shame to him" (Proverbs 18:13 NASB).

35. "A brother offended is harder to be won than a strong city, and contentions are like the bars of a citadel. With the fruit of a man's mouth his stomach will be satisfied; he will be satisfied with the product of his lips. Death and life are in the power of the tongue, and those who love it will eat its fruit" (Proverbs 18:19–21 NASB).

36. "A false witness will not go unpunished, and he who tells lies will not escape" (Proverbs 19:5 NASB).

37. "A false witness will not go unpunished, and he who tells lies will perish" (Proverbs 19:9 NASB).

38. "Keeping away from strife is an honor for a man, but any fool will quarrel" (Proverbs 20:3 NASB).

39. "He who goes about as a slanderer reveals secrets, therefore do not associate with a gossip. He who curses his father or his mother, his lamp will go out in time of darkness" (Proverbs 20:19–20 NASB).

40. "The acquisition of treasures by a lying tongue is a fleeting vapor, the pursuit of death" (Proverbs 21:6 NASB).

41. "He who guards his mouth and his tongue keeps himself from calamity" (Proverbs 21:23).

42. "He who guards his mouth and his tongue, guards his soul from troubles" (Proverbs 24:26 NASB).

43. "A false witness will perish, but the man who listens to the truth will speak forever" (Proverbs 24:28 NASB).

44. "Argue your case with your neighbor, and do not reveal the secret of another, or he who hears it will reproach you, and the evil report about you will not pass away. Like apples of gold in settings of silver is a word spoken in right circumstances. Like an earring of gold and an ornament of fine gold is a wise reprover to a listening ear" (Proverbs 25:9–12 NASB).

45. "Like clouds and wind without rain is a man who boasts of his gifts falsely. By forbearance a ruler may be persuaded, and a soft tongue breaks the bone" (Proverbs 25:14–15 NASB).

46. "Like a club and a sword and a sharp arrow is a man who bears false witness against his neighbor" (Proverbs 25:18 NASB).

47. "The north wind brings forth rain, and a backbiting tongue, an angry countenance" (Proverbs 25:23 NASB).

48. "Do not answer a fool according to his folly, or you will also be like him. Answer a fool as his folly deserves, that he not be wise in his own eyes" (Proverbs 26:4–5 NASB).

49. "Like a madman who throws firebrands, arrows and death, so is the man who deceives his neighbor, and says, 'Was I not joking?'" (Proverbs 26:18–19 NASB).

50. "For lack of wood the fire goes out, and where there is no whisperer, contention quiets down. Like charcoal to hot embers and wood to fire, so is a contentious man to kindle strife. The words of a whisperer are like dainty morsels, and they go down into the innermost parts of the body" (Proverbs 26:20–22 NASB).

51. "The words of a whisperer are like dainty morsels, and they go down into the innermost parts of the body. Like an earthen vessel overlaid with silver dross are burning lips and a wicked heart. He who hates disguises it with his lips, but he lays up deceit in his heart" (Proverbs 26:22–24 NASB).

52. "A lying tongue hates those it crushes, and a flattering mouth works ruin" (Proverbs 26:28 NASB).

53. "Let another praise you, and not your own mouth; a stranger, and not your own lips" (Proverbs 27:2 NASB).

54. "Better is open rebuke than love that is concealed" (Proverbs 27:5 NASB).

55. "He who blesses his friend with a loud voice early in the morning, it will be reckoned a curse to him" (Proverbs 27:14 NASB).

56. "He who rebukes a man will afterward find more favor than he who flatters with the tongue" (Proverbs 28:23 NASB).

57. "Do you see a man who is hasty in his words? There is more hope for a fool than for him" (Proverbs 29:20 NASB).

58. "If you have been foolish in exalting yourself or if you have plotted evil, put your hand on your mouth. For the churning of milk produces butter, and pressing the nose brings forth blood; so the churning of anger produces strife" (Proverbs 30:32–33 NASB).

59. "She opens her mouth in wisdom, and the teaching of kindness is on her tongue" (Proverbs 31:26 NASB).

◼ LIST #40

5 Passages That Relate to the Abortion Issue

The Bible does not directly use the word *abortion*. It does, however, make clear the importance of children to God and show that he has a plan for their lives.

1. "Now the word of the LORD came to me saying, before I formed you in the womb I knew you, and before you were born I consecrated you; I have appointed you a prophet to the nations" (Jeremiah 1:4–5 NASB).

2. "Your hands fashioned and made me altogether, and would You destroy me? Remember now, that You have made me as clay; and would You turn me into dust again? Did You not pour me out like milk and curdle me like cheese; clothe me with skin and flesh, and knit me together with bones and sinews? You have granted me life and loving kindness; and Your care has preserved my spirit" (Job 10:8–12 NASB).

3. "Behold, children are a gift of the LORD, the fruit of the womb is a reward. Like arrows in the hand of a warrior, so are the children of one's youth. How blessed is the man whose quiver is full of them; they will not be ashamed when they speak with their enemies in the gate" (Psalm 127:3–5 NASB).

4. "For You formed my inward parts; You wove me in my mother's womb. I will give thanks to You, for I am fearfully and wonderfully made; wonderful are Your works, and my soul knows it very well. My frame was

not hidden from You, when I was made in secret, and skillfully wrought in the depths of the earth; Your eyes have seen my unformed substance; and in Your book were all written the days that were ordained for me, when as yet there was not one of them" (Psalm 139:13–16 NASB).

5. "Thus says the LORD who made you and formed you from the womb, who will help you, do not fear, O Jacob My servant; and you Jeshurun whom I have chosen" (Isaiah 44:2 NASB).

LIST #41
26 Teachings about How to Live Forever

Having eternal life is possible for everyone who will exercise faith. Who wouldn't want to live with God forever? The Bible tells us how we can do just that.

1. "'Come now, and let us reason together,' says the LORD, 'Though your sins are as scarlet, they will be as white as snow; though they are red like crimson, they will be like wool'" (Isaiah 1:18 NASB).

2. "For I say to you that unless your righteousness surpasses that of the scribes and Pharisees, you will not enter the kingdom of heaven" (Matthew 5:20 NASB).

3. "For the gate is small and the way is narrow that leads to life, and there are few who find it" (Matthew 7:14 NASB).

4. "Do not fear those who kill the body but are unable to kill the soul; but rather fear Him who is able to destroy both soul and body in hell" (Matthew 10:28 NASB).

5. "Therefore everyone who confesses Me before men, I will also confess him before My Father who is in heaven. But whoever denies Me before men, I will also deny him before My Father who is in heaven" (Matthew 10:32–33 NASB).

6. "Come to Me, all who are weary and heavy-laden, and I will give you rest. Take My yoke upon you and learn from Me, for I am gentle and humble in heart, and you will find rest for your souls. For My yoke

is easy and My burden is light" (Matthew 11:28–30 NASB).

7. "You brood of vipers, how can you, being evil, speak what is good? For the mouth speaks out of that which fills the heart. The good man brings out of his good treasure what is good; and the evil man brings out of his evil treasure what is evil. But I tell you that every careless word that people speak, they shall give an accounting for it in the day of judgment. For by your words you will be justified, and by your words you will be condemned" (Matthew 12:34–37 NASB).

8. "For what will it profit a man if he gains the whole world and forfeits his soul? Or what will a man give in exchange for his soul?" (Matthew 16:26 NASB).

9. "Whoever seeks to keep his life will lose it, and whoever loses his life will preserve it" (Luke 17:33 NASB).

10. "For God so loved the world, that He gave His only begotten Son, that whoever believes in Him shall not perish, but have eternal life. For God did not send the Son into the world to judge the world, but that the world might be saved through Him. He who believes in Him is not judged; he who does not believe has been judged already, because he has not believed in the name of the only begotten Son of God" (John 3:16–18 NASB).

11. "He who believes in the Son has eternal life; but he who does not obey the Son will not see life, but the wrath of God abides on him" (John 3:36 NASB).

12. "But whoever drinks of the water that I will give him shall never thirst; but the water that I will give him will become in him a well of water springing up to eternal life" (John 4:14 NASB).

13. "My sheep hear My voice, and I know them, and they follow Me; and I give eternal life to them, and they will never perish; and no one will snatch them out of My hand. My Father, who has given them to Me, is greater than all; and no one is able to snatch them out of the Father's hand. I and the Father are one" (John 10:27–30 NASB).

14. "But these have been written so that you may believe that Jesus is the Christ, the Son of God; and that believing you may have life in His name" (John 20:31 NASB).

15. "And it shall be that everyone who calls on the name of the Lord will be saved" (Acts 2:21 NASB).

16. "And there is salvation in no one else; for there is no other name under heaven that has been given among men by which we must be saved" (Acts 4:12 NASB).

17. "For all have sinned and fall short of the glory of God" (Romans 3:23 NASB).

18. "Therefore, having been justified by faith, we have peace with God through our Lord Jesus Christ" (Romans 5:1 NASB).

19. "For the wages of sin is death, but the free gift of God is eternal life in Christ Jesus our Lord" (Romans 6:23 NASB).

20. ". . . if you confess with your mouth Jesus as Lord, and believe in your heart that God raised Him from the dead, you will be saved; for with the heart a person believes, resulting in righteousness, and with the mouth he confesses, resulting in salvation" (Romans 10:9–10 NASB).

21. "For whoever will call on the name of the Lord will be saved" (Romans 10:13 NASB).

22. "For we must all appear before the judgment seat of Christ, so that each one may be recompensed for his deeds in the body, according to what he has done, whether good or bad" (2 Corinthians 5:10 NASB).

23. "For by grace you have been saved through faith; and that not of yourselves, it is the gift of God; not as a result of works, so that no one may boast" (Ephesians 2:8–9 NASB).

24. "And inasmuch as it is appointed for men to die once and after this comes judgment, so Christ also, having been offered once to bear the sins of many, will appear a second time for salvation without reference to sin, to those who eagerly await Him" (Hebrews 9:27–28 NASB).

25. "If we confess our sins, He is faithful and righteous to forgive us our sins and to cleanse us from all unrighteousness" (1 John 1:9 NASB).

26. "Behold, I stand at the door and knock; if anyone hears My voice and opens the door, I will come in to him and will dine with him, and he with Me" (Revelation 3:20 NASB).

LIST #42
11 Helps for Worrywarts

Worry can't change the course of events, but it can prevent any present enjoyment. It drains our peace, joy, and happiness. But the Bible tells us we need not worry: only trust God.

1. "Have I not commanded you? Be strong and courageous! Do not tremble or be dismayed, for the LORD your God is with you wherever you go" (Joshua 1:9 NASB).

2. "Even though I walk through the valley of the shadow of death, I fear no evil, for You are with me; Your rod and Your staff, they comfort me" (Psalm 23:4 NASB).

3. "For my father and my mother have forsaken me, but the LORD will take me up" (Psalm 27:10 NASB).

4. "For He will give His angels charge concerning you, to guard you in all your ways" (Psalm 91:11 NASB).

5. "Do not fear, for I am with you; do not anxiously look about you, for I am your God I will strengthen you, surely I will help you, surely I will uphold you with My righteous right hand" (Isaiah 41:10 NASB).

6. "But now, thus says the LORD, your Creator, O Jacob, and He who formed you, O Israel, 'Do not fear, for I have redeemed you; I have called you by name; you are Mine! When you pass through the waters, I will be with you; and through the rivers, they will not overflow you. When you walk through the fire, you will not be scorched, nor will the flame burn you'" (Isaiah 43:1–2 NASB).

7. "And lo, I am with you always, even to the end of the age" (Matthew 28:20 NASB).

8. "Make sure that your character is free from the love of money, being content with what you have; for He Himself has said, 'I will never desert you, nor will I ever forsake you,' so that we confidently say, 'The Lord is my helper, I will not be afraid. What will man do to me?'" (Hebrews 13:5–6 NASB).

9. "For I am the LORD your God, who upholds your right hand, who says to you, do not fear, I will help you" (Isaiah 41:13 NASB).

10. "For this reason I say to you, do not be worried about your life, as to what you will eat or what you will drink; nor for your body, as to what you will put on. Is not life more than food, and the body more than clothing? Look at the birds of the air, that they do not sow, nor reap nor gather into barns, and yet your heavenly Father feeds them. Are you not worth much more than they? And who of you by being worried can add a single hour to his life? And why are you worried about clothing? Observe how the lilies of the field grow; they do not toil nor do they spin, yet I say to you that not even Solomon in all his glory clothed himself like one of these. But if God so clothes the grass of the field, which is alive today and tomorrow is thrown into the furnace, will He not much more clothe you? You of little faith! Do not worry then, saying, 'What will we eat?' or 'What will we drink?' or 'What will we wear for clothing?' For the Gentiles eagerly seek all these things; for your heavenly Father knows that you need all these things. But seek first His kingdom and His righteousness, and all these things will be added to

you. So do not worry about tomorrow; for tomorrow will care for itself. Each day has enough trouble of its own" (Matthew 6:25–34 NASB).

11. "Therefore humble yourselves under the mighty hand of God, that He may exalt you at the proper time, casting all your anxiety on Him, because He cares for you" (1 Peter 5:6–7 NASB).

■ LIST #43
244 Topical Trivia Words

The Bible seems to place an emphasis on some topics more than others. Topping the list in frequency are mentions of the Lord, God, sons, kings, man, houses, and fathers.

Word Occurrences in the Bible

Adam—33	Bald(ness)—21	Boy(s)—15
Adoption—5	Baptism—22	Bracelet(s)—8
Adornment—1	Bath(ing)—8	Braided—9
Adulterer—3	Beard(s)—20	Bread—352
Adulteress—5	Beautiful—53	Bride—18
Adultery—44	Beauty—50	Bridegroom—28
Aged—9	Believers—6	Brother(s)—545
Ancestors—2	Belly—18	Busybody—1
Angel(s)—299	Betrothed—14	Butter—3
Anger / angry—327	Birth(s)—54	Caring—2
Anxious—8	Bitterness—21	Character—6
Apples—10	Blame—4	Child—182
Archangel—2	Blessing(s)—97	Children—135
Argue—1	Body—229	Christ—612
Atonement—102	Born—151	Christian(s)—8
Babies / baby—5	Bowls—72	Church—96

Circumcision—34

Cleanliness—1

Cloth—18

Clothing—49

Coat(s)—8

Concubine(s)—24

Cook(ing)—7

Courage—20

Cousin—1

Covet—10

Cucumbers—2

Cup(s)—77

Dancing—6

Daughter(s)—556

Daughter-in-law—17

Death—463

Demon(s)—69

Depression—1

Devil—36

Dinner—5

Discipline(d)—4

Dish(es)—9

Divorce(d)—28

Doubt(s)—4

Dress—1

Earrings—12

Eating—32

Egg(s)—9

Encourage(ment)—5

Engagement—13

Envious—6

Eunuch—10

Eve—4

Evil—488

Exercise—8

Eye(s)—610

Faith—281

Family—362

Father(s)—1,484

Father-in-law—26

Fear(s)—394

Feast(s)—185

Feet—244

Female—85

Festival(s)—4

Flattery—2

Flowers—10

Food—212

Forgive(ness)—69

Friend(s)—123

Friendship—2

Fruit(s)—213

Garden(s)—71

Garlic—1

Garment(s)—214

Generous—8

Girl(s)—31

Give / giving—948

God—4,533

Gossip—10

Grain—256

Grandchildren—4

Grandfather—3

Grandmother—2

Grapes—39

Gray hair / gray headed—6

Greed—3

Grumbling—1

Hair—77

Handsome—5

Happiness / happy—29

Harlot—79

Heaven—540

Hell—32

Holiness—35

Holy—649

Home(s)—74

Hope—149

Hostility—1

House—1,755

Humility—14

Husband(s)—143

Immoral(ity)—33

Incense—148

Infant(s)—11

Intermarriage—1

Jar—6

Jealousy—33

Jesus—1,153

Kind(ness)—115

King(s)—2,720

Kiss—20

Knee(s)—37

Knife—5

Labor—109

Lamp(s)—73

Laugh(ed)—22

Lazy—16

Leeks—1

Liar(s)—17

Life—520

Linen—106

Lip(s)—120

Loom—4

Lord—5,000

Love—387

Maid(en)—21

Male—164

Man—2,111

Market—3

Marriage(s)—9

Meals—25

Melons—1

Men—1,610

Milk—51

Mirror(s)—6

Miscarriage / miscarry—2

Money—150

Mother(s)—245

Mother-in-law—15

Music—23

Necklace(s)—4

Needle—3

Neighbor(s)—123

Obedience / obey—137

Oil—225

Old age—14

Onions—1

Orphan(s)—4

Pain—29

Parent(s)—22

Patience—25

Peace—407

Perfume—2

Pitcher(s)—24

Pot(s)—35

Praise—268

Pray(er)—317

Pride—54

Prodigal—1

Prophetess—8

Prostitute—3

Punish—47

Quarrel—8

Queen(s)—60

Reconcile(d)—13

Respect—17

Rewards—4

Rings—61

Robe(s)—66

Rumor(s)—3

Sandal(s)—35

Satan—25

Selfish—6

Serve / service / serving—351

Sew(ed)—3

Share / sharing—21

Shoe—2

Sick(ness)—95

Silk—3

Sin(s)—668

Sing(ing)—143

Sister(s)—129

Sister-in-law—5

Skirt(s)—7

Slander—4

Smile—3

Son(s)—3,749

Son-in-law—13

Strength—231

Submission / submit—20

Talebearer—6

Tears—37

Temptation—13

Thanksgiving—39

Thought(s)—104

Tongue—115

Trust—130

Virgin(s)—66

Wash(ing)—97

Water—463

Wean(ed)—12

Weave—5

Wedding—14

Widow(s)—90

Wife / wives—532

Wine—238

Wisdom / wise—470

Woman—405

Womb—75

Women—194

Word of God—51

Worry—11

Wound(s)—36

Youth(s)—74

LIST #44
15 Bad Hair Days

Everyone occasionally has a really bad hair day. Here are some people whose hair "challenges" are recorded in the Bible for all time.

1. "Now the first came forth red, all over like a hairy garment; and they named him Esau" (Genesis 25:25 NASB).

2. "Then Moses said to Aaron and to his sons Eleazar and Ithamar, 'Do not uncover your heads nor tear your clothes, so that you will not die and that He will not become wrathful against all the congregation. But your kinsmen, the whole house of Israel, shall bewail the burning which the LORD has brought about'" (Leviticus 10:6 NASB).

3. "All the days of his vow of separation no razor shall pass over his head. He shall be holy until the days are fulfilled for which he separated himself to the LORD; he shall let the locks of hair on his head grow long" (Numbers 6:5 NASB).

4. "She made him sleep on her knees, and called for a man and had him shave off the seven locks of his hair. Then she began to afflict him, and his strength left him" (Judges 16:19 NASB).

5. "When he cut the hair of his head (and it was at the end of every year that he cut it, for it was heavy on him so he cut it), he weighed the hair of his head at 200 shekels by the king's weight" (2 Samuel 14:26 NASB).

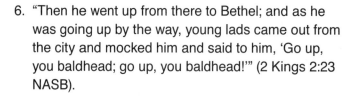

6. "Then he went up from there to Bethel; and as he was going up by the way, young lads came out from the city and mocked him and said to him, 'Go up, you baldhead; go up, you baldhead!'" (2 Kings 2:23 NASB).

7. "When I heard about this matter, I tore my garment and my robe, and pulled some of the hair from my head and my beard, and sat down appalled" (Ezra 9:3 NASB).

8. "So I contended with them and cursed them and struck some of them and pulled out their hair, and made them swear by God, 'You shall not give your daughters to their sons, nor take of their daughters for your sons or for yourselves'" (Nehemiah 13:25 NASB).

9. "Then Job arose and tore his robe and shaved his head, and he fell to the ground and worshiped" (Job 1:20 NASB).

10. "Now it will come about that instead of sweet perfume there will be putrefaction; instead of a belt, a rope; instead of well-set hair, a plucked-out scalp; instead of fine clothes, a donning of sackcloth; and branding instead of beauty" (Isaiah 3:24 NASB).

11. "As for you, son of man, take a sharp sword; take and use it as a barber's razor on your head and beard Then take scales for weighing and divide the hair" (Ezekiel 5:1 NASB).

12. "He stretched out the form of a hand and caught me by a lock of my head; and the Spirit lifted me up between earth and heaven and brought me in the visions of God to Jerusalem, to the entrance of the north gate of the inner court, where the seat of the

idol of jealousy, which provokes to jealousy, was located" (Ezekiel 8:3 NASB).

13. "Immediately the word concerning Nebuchadnezzar was fulfilled; and he was driven away from mankind and began eating grass like cattle, and his body was drenched with the dew of heaven until his hair had grown like eagles' feathers and his nails like birds' claws" (Daniel 4:33 NASB).

14. "And standing behind Him at His feet, weeping, she began to wet His feet with her tears, and kept wiping them with the hair of her head, and kissing His feet and anointing them with the perfume" (Luke 7:38 NASB).

15. "Therefore do this that we tell you. We have four men who are under a vow; take them and purify yourself along with them, and pay their expenses so that they may shave their heads; and all will know that there is nothing to the things which they have been told about you, but that you yourself also walk orderly, keeping the Law" (Acts 21:23–24 NASB).

LIST #45

9 Passages to Consider in Seeking God's Will

Finding the will of God may not be as difficult as one would expect. Consider some scriptures related to this important subject:

1. "Be still, and know that I am God; I will be exalted among the nations, I will be exalted in the earth" (Psalm 46:10).

2. "He who dwells in the shelter of the Most High will rest in the shadow of the Almighty. I will say of the LORD, 'He is my refuge and my fortress, my God, in whom I trust'" (Psalm 91:1–2).

3. "Trust in the LORD with all your heart and lean not on your own understanding; in all your ways acknowledge him, and he will make your paths straight" (Proverbs 3:5–6).

4. "Each one should test his own actions. Then he can take pride in himself, without comparing himself to somebody else, for each one should carry his own load" (Galatians 6:4–5).

5. "In him we were also chosen, having been predestined according to the plan of him who works out everything in conformity with the purpose of his will" (Ephesians 1:11).

6. "As you have always obeyed—not only in my presence, but now much more in my absence—continue to work out your salvation with fear and

trembling, for it is God who works in you to will and to act according to his good purpose" (Philippians 2:12–13).

7. "It is God's will that you should be sanctified: that you should avoid sexual immorality; that each of you should learn to control his own body in a way that is holy and honorable, not in passionate lust like the heathen, who do not know God; and that in this matter no one should wrong his brother or take advantage of him. The Lord will punish men for all such sins, as we have already told you and warned you. For God did not call us to be impure, but to live a holy life. Therefore, he who rejects this instruction does not reject man but God, who gives you his Holy Spirit" (1 Thessalonians 4:3–8).

8. "Be joyful always; pray continually; give thanks in all circumstances, for this is God's will for you in Christ Jesus" (1 Thessalonians 5:16–18).

9. "It is better, if it is God's will, to suffer for doing good than for doing evil" (1 Peter 3:17).

■ LIST #46

32 Miscellaneous Bible References to Women

The Bible describes women (some figurative) in various circumstances.

1. Daughters of kings (honored women)—Psalm 45:9

2. Daughters like pillars carved to adorn a palace—Psalm 144:12

3. Woman who shows no discretion—Proverbs 11:22

4. Wise woman, foolish woman—Proverbs 14:1

5. Quarrelsome wife—Proverbs 19:13; 21:9; 25:24; 27:15

6. Adulterous woman—Proverbs 30:20

7. Unloved woman who is married—Proverbs 30:21–23

8. Maidservant who displaces her mistress—Proverbs 30:23

9. Wife of noble character—Proverbs 31:10

10. Woman who is like merchant ships, bringing food from afar—Proverbs 31:14

11. Woman who fears the Lord—Proverbs 31:30

12. Woman who is a snare—Ecclesiastes 7:26

13. The Shulammite—Song of Solomon 6:13–14

14. Complacent women—Isaiah 32:9–11

15. Woman who forgets her baby at her breast—Isaiah 49:15

16. Mothers who comfort their children—Isaiah 66:13

17. Daughters of people who prophesy out of their own imaginations—Ezekiel 13:17

18. Women who sew magic charms on their wrists—Ezekiel 13:18

19. Woman with seven husbands—Matthew 22:25–32; Luke 20:27–38

20. Women grinding with a hand mill—Matthew 24:41

21. Ten virgins—Matthew 25:1–7

22. Woman who lost her silver coin—Luke 15:8–9

23. Persistent widow—Luke 18:1–8

24. Woman giving birth—John 16:21

25. Wife who is not a believer—1 Corinthians 7:12

26. Women in the churches—1 Corinthians 14:34

27. Women who profess to worship God—1 Timothy 2:9

28. Younger widows—1 Timothy 5:11

29. Women who become idlers and gossips and busybodies—1 Timothy 5:13

30. Weak-willed women—2 Timothy 3:6

31. Older women, younger women—Titus 2:3–5

32. Chosen lady—2 John 1–3

◼ LIST #47
52 Passages about Weeping and Wailing

Tears are sometimes a sign of joy, but in most cases they're an indication of pain, suffering, or sorrow. Listed below are some in the Bible who shed tears.

1. Hagar—Genesis 21:14–16
2. Abraham—Genesis 23:2
3. Esau—Genesis 27:38
4. Jacob—Genesis 29:11
5. Joseph—Genesis 43:30
6. Benjamin—Genesis 45:14
7. Baby Moses—Exodus 2:6
8. The Israelites who craved other food—Numbers 11:10
9. The children of Israel at Bokim—Judges 2:4
10. Samson's wife—Judges 14:16
11. Orpah and Ruth—Ruth 1:14
12. Hannah—1 Samuel 1:8
13. People of Gibeah—1 Samuel 11:4
14. David and Jonathan—1 Samuel 20:41
15. Saul—1 Samuel 24:16
16. David and his men—1 Samuel 30:4
17. Michal's husband Paltiel—2 Samuel 3:14–16

18. David, his sons, and all his servants—2 Samuel 13:36

19. Elisha—2 Kings 8:10–11

20. Jehoash—2 Kings 13:14

21. Hezekiah—2 Kings 20:3

22. Josiah, king of Judah—2 Chronicles 34:26–27

23. Older priests, Levites, and family heads—Ezra 3:12

24. Ezra and the crowd—Ezra 10:1

25. Nehemiah—Nehemiah 1:4

26. All the people—Nehemiah 8:9

27. Jews in the Persian kingdom—Esther 4:3

28. Esther—Esther 8:3

29. Eliphaz, Bildad, and Zophar—Job 2:11–12

30. Job—Job 16:20

31. Isaiah—Isaiah 22:4

32. Rachel—Jeremiah 31:15

33. Ishmael, son of Nethaniah—Jeremiah 41:6

34. Jeremiah—Lamentations 2:11

35. Women mourning for Tammuz—Ezekiel 8:14

36. Peter—Matthew 26:75

37. Mourners for Jairus's daughter—Mark 5:38

38. Those who had been with Jesus—Mark 16:10

39. The widow of Nain—Luke 7:12–13

40. Woman who had lived a sinful life—Luke 7:37–38

41. Daughters of Jerusalem—Luke 23:28

42. Mary, Martha's sister—John 11:32–33

43. Jesus—John 11:35

44. Mary Magdalene—John 20:11

45. The widows Dorcas had helped—Acts 9:39

46. Paul—Acts 20:17–19

47. Ephesian elders—Acts 20:37

48. Christians in Caesarea, Paul's friends—Acts 21:12–13

49. Timothy—2 Timothy 1:4

50. Melchizedek—Hebrews 5:7

51. John—Revelation 5:4

52. All who make their living from the sea—Revelation 18:19

⬛ LIST #48
19 Helps in Choosing to Obey God

Charles H. Spurgeon said, "Some temptations come to the industrious, but all temptations attack the idle." R. E. Phillips said, "When fleeing temptation, don't leave a forwarding address." Resisting temptation and choosing to obey God can be difficult—but it's possible. Here's what the Bible says about it.

1. "What I am commanding you today is not too difficult for you or beyond your reach. It is not up in heaven, so that you have to ask, 'Who will ascend into heaven to get it and proclaim it to us so we may obey it?' Nor is it beyond the sea, so that you have to ask, 'Who will cross the sea to get it and proclaim it to us so we may obey it?' No, the word is very near you; it is in your mouth and in your heart so you may obey it.

   "See, I set before you today life and prosperity, death and destruction. For I command you today to love the LORD your God, to walk in his ways, and to keep his commands, decrees and laws; then you will live and increase, and the LORD your God will bless you in the land you are entering to possess" (Deuteronomy 30:11–16).

2. "The fear of the LORD is the beginning of wisdom; all who follow his precepts have good understanding. To him belongs eternal praise" (Psalm 111:10).

3. "Blessed are they who keep his statutes and seek him with all their heart" (Psalm 119:2).

4. "Now all has been heard; here is the conclusion of the matter: Fear God and keep his commandments, for this is the whole duty of man. For God will bring every deed into judgment, including every hidden thing, whether it is good or evil" (Ecclesiastes 12:13–14).

5. "No one can serve two masters. Either he will hate the one and love the other, or he will be devoted to the one and despise the other. You cannot serve both God and Money" (Matthew 6:24).

6. "If you love me, you will obey what I command" (John 14:15).

7. "Whoever has my commands and obeys them, he is the one who loves me. He who loves me will be loved by my Father, and I too will love him and show myself to him" (John 14:21).

8. "Don't you know that when you offer yourselves to someone to obey him as slaves, you are slaves to the one whom you obey—whether you are slaves to sin, which leads to death, or to obedience, which leads to righteousness? But thanks be to God that, though you used to be slaves to sin, you wholeheartedly obeyed the form of teaching to which you were entrusted. You have been set free from sin and have become slaves to righteousness" (Romans 6:16–18).

9. "Dear friends, if our hearts do not condemn us, we have confidence before God and receive from him anything we ask, because we obey his commands and do what pleases him. And this is his command: to believe in the name of his Son, Jesus Christ, and to love one another as he commanded us. Those who

obey his commands live in him, and he in them. And this is how we know that he lives in us: We know it by the Spirit he gave us" (1 John 3:21–24).

10. "Unless the LORD had given me help, I would soon have dwelt in the silence of death. When I said, 'My foot is slipping,' your love, O LORD, supported me. When anxiety was great within me, your consolation brought joy to my soul" (Psalm 94:17–19).

11. "Watch and pray so that you will not fall into temptation. The spirit is willing, but the body is weak" (Matthew 26:41).

12. "If you think you are standing firm, be careful that you don't fall! No temptation has seized you except what is common to man. And God is faithful; he will not let you be tempted beyond what you can bear. But when you are tempted, he will also provide a way out so that you can stand up under it" (1 Corinthians 10:12–13).

13. "Because he himself suffered when he was tempted, he is able to help those who are being tempted" (Hebrews 2:18).

14. "Since we have a great high priest who has gone through the heavens, Jesus the Son of God, let us hold firmly to the faith we profess. For we do not have a high priest who is unable to sympathize with our weaknesses, but we have one who has been tempted in every way, just as we are—yet was without sin. Let us then approach the throne of grace with confidence, so that we may receive mercy and find grace to help us in our time of need" (Hebrews 4:14–16).

15. "Blessed is the man who perseveres under trial, because when he has stood the test, he will receive the crown of life that God has promised to those who love him. When tempted, no one should say, 'God is tempting me.' For God cannot be tempted by evil, nor does he tempt anyone; but each one is tempted when, by his own evil desire, he is dragged away and enticed. Then, after desire has conceived, it gives birth to sin; and sin, when it is full-grown, gives birth to death" (James 1:12–15).

16. "In this you greatly rejoice, though now for a little while you may have had to suffer grief in all kinds of trials. These have come so that your faith—of greater worth than gold, which perishes even though refined by fire—may be proved genuine and may result in praise, glory and honor when Jesus Christ is revealed" (1 Peter 1:6–7).

17. "The Lord knows how to rescue godly men from trials and to hold the unrighteous for the day of judgment, while continuing their punishment" (2 Peter 2:9).

18. "You, dear children, are from God and have overcome them, because the one who is in you is greater than the one who is in the world" (1 John 4:4).

19. "To him who is able to keep you from falling and to present you before his glorious presence without fault and with great joy—to the only God our Savior be glory, majesty, power and authority, through Jesus Christ our Lord, before all ages, now and forevermore! Amen" (Jude 24–25).

■ LIST #49
12 Bible Blessings

Learning to develop a grateful spirit for God's gifts is a sign of spiritual health. As Charles Dickens once said, "Reflect on your present blessings, of which every man has many, not on your past misfortunes, of which all men have some."

1. "The LORD bless you and keep you; the LORD make his face shine upon you and be gracious to you; the LORD turn his face toward you and give you peace" (Numbers 6:24–26).

2. "Grace and peace to you from God our Father and from the Lord Jesus Christ" (Romans 1:7).

3. "The God of peace be with you all. Amen" (Romans 15:33).

4. "May the grace of our Lord Jesus Christ be with you all. Amen" (Romans 16:24 NKJV).

5. "Peace to the brothers, and love with faith from God the Father and the Lord Jesus Christ. Grace to all who love our Lord Jesus Christ with an undying love" (Ephesians 6:23–24).

6. "May the Lord of peace himself give you peace at all times and in every way. The Lord be with all of you" (2 Thessalonians 3:16).

7. "Grace, mercy and peace from God the Father and Christ Jesus our Lord" (1 Timothy 1:2).

8. "The Lord be with your spirit. Grace be with you" (2 Timothy 4:22).

9. "May the God of peace, who through the blood of the eternal covenant brought back from the dead our Lord Jesus, that great Shepherd of the sheep, equip you with everything good for doing his will, and may he work in us what is pleasing to him, through Jesus Christ, to whom be glory for ever and ever. Amen" (Hebrews 13:20–21).

10. "Peace to all of you who are in Christ" (1 Peter 5:14).

11. "Grace and peace be yours in abundance through the knowledge of God and of Jesus our Lord" (2 Peter 1:2).

12. "Grace and peace to you from him who is, and who was, and who is to come, and from the seven spirits before his throne, and from Jesus Christ, who is the faithful witness, the firstborn from the dead, and the ruler of the kings of the earth" (Revelation 1:4–5).

■ LIST #50
101 Bible Trivia Questions

Did you know that a man in the Bible was eaten by worms? That the Bible talks about nose jewelry? That people rubbed babies with salt? If you enjoy Bible trivia, here are some fun questions for you.

1. What holiday did God command the children of Israel to celebrate using bitter herbs? *Passover (Numbers 9:11–13)*

2. If someone gave his cloak as a pledge for a loan, when was the lender required to return it? *By sunset (Exodus 22:26–27)*

3. What did Naboth and Stephen have in common? *Both were stoned to death (1 Kings 21:13; Acts 6:12; 7:58).*

4. Whom did God instruct to take off his shoes? *Moses and Joshua (Exodus 3:5; Joshua 5:15)*

5. Who hammered a tent peg through a man's head? *Jael (Judges 4:21)*

6. Which judge stabbed King Eglon, a man so rotund that the dagger was engulfed in fat? *Ehud (Judges 3:12–22)*

7. Who dropped a millstone on Abimelech's head? *A woman (Judges 9:52–53)*

8. Which Greek gods did the people of Lystra believe Paul and Barnabas were after they healed a lame man? *Zeus and Hermes (Acts 14:11–12)*

9. What did Goliath and John the Baptist have in common? *Both were beheaded (1 Samuel 17:51; Matthew 14:6–12).*

10. How was Melchizedek greater than Abraham? *He blessed Abraham, and "without doubt the lesser person is blessed by the greater" (Hebrews 7:1–7).*

11. Who commanded the sun to stand still—and it did? *Joshua (Joshua 10:12–13)*

12. What odd thing happened to Elizabeth's baby when Mary greeted her? *It leaped in her womb (Luke 1:41).*

13. Whose mother scolded him, saying: "Son, why have you treated us like this? Your father and I have been anxiously searching for you?" *Jesus's (Luke 2:41–52)*

14. Which prophet was told not to mourn his wife's sudden death? *Ezekiel (Ezekiel 24:15–18)*

15. Which prophet was told to marry an adulteress? *Hosea (Hosea 1:2–3)*

16. Who slept at the feet of her future husband before they were married? *Ruth (Ruth 3:7–14)*

17. Whose daughters got their father drunk and had sex with him? *Lot's (Genesis 19:30–36)*

18. What evil queen was eaten by dogs? *Jezebel (2 Kings 9:34–37)*

19. What did Samson, King Saul, Saul's armor bearer, Ahithophel, Zimri, and Judas have in common? *They committed suicide (Judges 16:30; 1 Samuel 31:4–5; 2 Samuel 17:23; 1 Kings 16:18; Matthew 27:5).*

20. What did Haman and Judas have in common? *Both were hanged (Esther 7:10; Matthew 27:5).*

21. What was the name of the woman Paul restored to life? *Dorcas or Tabitha (Acts 9:36–41)*

22. Which judge sacrificed his own daughter rather than break his vow? *Jephthah (Judges 11:30–40)*

23. What wicked queen destroyed most of her own royal family? *Athaliah (2 Kings 11:1–2)*

24. What did an Israelite man not have to do for the first year of his marriage? *Go to war or have any other duty laid on him (Deuteronomy 24:5)*

25. What man went to sleep single and woke up to find he had a wife? *Adam (Genesis 2:21–24)*

26. What were the names of the husband and wife who died because they lied to the Holy Spirit? *Ananias and Sapphira (Acts 5:1–11)*

27. How many women can you name who had more than one husband? *Tamar, Samson's wife, Ruth, Michal, the hypothetical woman described by the Sadducees, and the woman at the well (Genesis 38:6–10; Judges 14:20; Ruth 4:10, 13; 2 Samuel 3:13–16; Mark 12:18–25; John 4:6–19)*

28. What innocent man was put in prison when a woman accused him of attempted rape? *Joseph (Genesis 39:7–20)*

29. Who called Moses a bridegroom of blood? *His wife, Zipporah (Exodus 4:25–26)*

30. What man of God lost his head for criticizing a king? *John the Baptist (Matthew 14:3–12)*

31. Why was Herod eaten by worms? *He accepted praise as a god instead of giving praise to God (Acts 12:23).*

32. Who was tossed out a window to her death? *Queen Jezebel (2 Kings 9:30–33)*

33. Who escaped arrest by being lowered in a basket from a window in the Damascus city wall? *Paul (2 Corinthians 11:32–33)*

34. Jesus said no one born was greater than what man? *John the Baptist (Matthew 11:11)*

35. How was King David kept warm when he was an old man? *A beautiful young woman, Abishag, lay beside David (1 Kings 1:2–4).*

36. Whose daughter-in-law named her son Ichabod on the day her husband, brother-in-law, and father-in-law all died? *Eli's (1 Samuel 4:21)*

37. What did Lazarus and Tabitha have in common? *Both were raised from the dead (John 11:43–44; Acts 9:40–41).*

38. Which prophet was put into a cistern, in which he sank in the mud? *Jeremiah (Jeremiah 38:6)*

39. How many rivers flowed out of the Garden of Eden? *Four: the Pishon, the Gihon, the Tigris, and the Euphrates (Genesis 2:10–14)*

40. What was the name of the person who wrote down the epistle to the Romans for Paul? *Tertius (Romans 16:22)*

41. When the seventh seal is opened, how long does the book of Revelation say there will be silence in heaven? *About half an hour (Revelation 8:1)*

42. What was the name of the blind man Bartimaeus's father? *Timaeus: Bar means "son of" (Mark 10:46).*

43. What fruit was to be embroidered around the hem of the priests' garments? *Pomegranates (Exodus 28:34)*

44. What Bible man lived in the land of Uz? *Job (Job 1:1)*

45. What special meaning does the word *Ebenezer* have? *"Thus far has the LORD helped us" (1 Samuel 7:12).*

46. Who fell asleep during one of Paul's sermons and fell to his death? *A young man named Eutychus (Acts 20:9)*

47. Why did God's anger burn against Uzzah when he tried to steady the ark of God? *No one but specified Levites were allowed to touch the Ark; God punished his irreverent act (2 Samuel 6:6–7).*

48. What is the shortest verse in the Old Testament? *"Eber, Peleg, Rue" (1 Chronicles 1:25)*

49. What unique characteristic was shared by the Zamzummites, Rephaites, and Anakites? *Extreme height (Deuteronomy 2:20–21)*

50. Who was the first archer mentioned in the Bible? *Ishmael (Genesis 21:20)*

51. Which Bible person referred to himself as a dead dog? *Mephibosheth (2 Samuel 9:6–8)*

52. What four colored horses are mentioned in the book of Revelation? *A white horse, a fiery red horse, a black horse, and a pale horse (Revelation 6:1–8)*

53. What Canaanite king slept in a bed that was more than six feet wide and more than thirteen feet long? *Og, king of Bashan (Deuteronomy 3:11)*

54. What little boy was hidden in the temple for six years to escape the wrath of his wicked grandmother? *Joash (2 Kings 11:1–2)*

55. What city was Goliath from? *Gath (1 Samuel 17:4)*

56. Who spoke 3,000 proverbs and wrote 1,005 songs?
    Solomon (1 Kings 4:32)

57. What was the name of Jeremiah's secretary? *Baruch*
    (Jeremiah 36:4)

58. Who told Job that the hair on his body stood up on end
    when he saw a spirit? *Eliphaz the Temanite (Job 4:1, 15)*

59. What son of Gideon murdered his seventy half-brothers?
    Abimelech (Judges 9:4–5)

60. Who wept when he kissed his sweetheart for the first
    time? *Jacob (Genesis 29:11)*

61. Who received a sandal along with the privilege of
    marrying his relative's widow? *Boaz (Ruth 4:7–10)*

62. Whose son was dropped by his nurse, resulting in the
    boy's being lame for life? *Jonathan's (2 Samuel 4:4)*

63. Name a lawyer mentioned in the Bible. *Zenas (Titus 3:13)*

64. What king ate grass like cattle? *Nebuchadnezzar*
    (Daniel 4:33)

65. What man had breath that was offensive to his wife?
    Job (Job 19:17)

66. What prophet ate a scroll that tasted sweet like
    honey? *Ezekiel (Ezekiel 2:9; 3:3)*

67. What is the shortest chapter in the Bible? *Psalm 117,*
    with only two verses

68. Who was told by an angel to eat a scroll that tasted
    sweet as honey in his mouth but turned his stomach
    sour? *John (Revelation 10:10)*

69. What prophet walked around naked and barefoot for three years? *Isaiah (Isaiah 20:3)*

70. What incredible feat did Samson, David, and Benaiah all manage to accomplish? *Killing a lion (Judges 14:5–6; 1 Samuel 17:34–36; 2 Samuel 23:20)*

71. Which one of David's mighty men killed eight hundred enemies with his spear in one encounter? *Josheb-Basshebeth (2 Samuel 23:8)*

72. What implement did Israel's judge Shamgar use to strike down six hundred Philistines? *An oxgoad (Judges 3:31)*

73. Who cursed the day he was born, wishing he had died at birth? *Job (Job 3:2–3, 11, 16)*

74. What well-known judge in Israel was a polygamist? *Gideon (Judges 8:30)*

75. What did the Philistines place in the ark of the Lord before returning it to the Israelites? *Five gold tumors and five gold rats (1 Samuel 6:1–5)*

76. Who was the first drunkard recorded in the Bible? *Noah (Genesis 9:20–21)*

77. Mispronouncing what one word caused 42,000 men to be killed? *Shibboleth (Judges 12:5–6)*

78. Who drew his bow and shot King Joram between the shoulders, piercing his heart? *Jehu (2 Kings 9:24)*

79. What Canaanite king fed scraps under his table to seventy kings with their thumbs cut off? *Adoni-Bezek (Judges 1:7)*

80. What was Queen Esther's Hebrew name? *Hadassah (Esther 2:7)*

81. What did James, Joseph, Simon, and Judas have in common? *They were Jesus's brothers (Matthew 13:55).*

82. What king of Judah burned his son as a sacrifice? *Ahaz (2 Kings 16:2–3)*

83. Which Israelite judge caught three hundred foxes, tied them tail to tail in pairs, fastened a burning torch to each pair, and let them loose to burn up the Philistines' grain fields? *Samson (Judges 15:4–5)*

84. In Proverbs, Solomon talked about four creatures that are small but extremely wise. How many can you name? *Ants, coneys, locusts, and lizards (Proverbs 30:24–28)*

85. In Ecclesiastes 9:4 the teacher said that a living dog is better than a dead what? *Lion (Ecclesiastes 9:4)*

86. What king of Israel set fire to his own palace and died in the flames? *Zimri (1 Kings 16:18)*

87. Before Delilah had it cut, how did Samson wear his hair? *In seven braids (Judges 16:19–20)*

88. By what three other names was Jerusalem known? *Jebus, Salem, and Zion (Judges 19:10; Psalm 76:2)*

89. How much money did each of the Philistine rulers offer Delilah to find out the secret of Samson's strength? *Eleven hundred shekels of silver (Judges 16:5)*

90. What did Michal, David's wife, place in his bed to trick those who sought to kill him? *An idol covered with a garment, and goat's hair at its head (1 Samuel 19:12–16)*

91. What man does the Bible quote as saying, "I have escaped with only the skin of my teeth"? *Job (Job 19:20)*

92. What prophet lay on his right side for forty days? *Ezekiel (Ezekiel 4:6)*

93. What did idol worshipers call the bronze snake of Moses? *Nehushtan (2 Kings 18:4)*

94. Who killed his master, King Ben-Hadad of Aram, by spreading a thick, wet cloth over his face? *Hazael (2 Kings 8:14–15)*

95. Who demanded the heads of Ahab's seventy sons in exchange for peace? *Jehu (2 Kings 10:1–7)*

96. What king of Israel fell on his sword before being beheaded, fastened to a city wall, cremated, and finally buried? *Saul (1 Samuel 31:4–13)*

97. What new king of Israel was badly advised to tell his subjects, "My little finger is thicker than my father's waist"? *Rehoboam (2 Chronicles 10:10)*

98. What king of Judah was afflicted with an incurable disease of the bowels? *Jehoram (2 Chronicles 21:18–19)*

99. What country seized David's sympathy delegation, shaved off half of their beards, and cut off their garments at the buttocks? *Ammon (2 Samuel 10:4)*

100. What once-good king of Judah was afflicted with a disease in his feet? *Asa (2 Chronicles 16:12)*

101. What Bible prophet protested at God's instruction to bake his food using human excrement for fuel? *Ezekiel (Ezekiel 4:15)*

BOB PHILLIPS

is a marriage, family, and child counselor who has written more than eighty books, including *Find It in the Bible, The Delicate Art of Dancing with Porcupines* and *Anger Is a Choice*. He has presented leadership seminars worldwide in nineteen countries and has appeared on a number of TV and radio programs across the United States. Bob and his wife live in south central California and have two daughters and three grandsons.